SCI-FI
SCENES
········· AND ·········
MONSTER DREAMS

16 COMEDY SCENES FOR STUDENT ACTORS

JAN PETERSON EWEN

MERIWETHER PUBLISHING
A division of Pioneer Drama Service, Inc.
Denver, Colorado

Meriwether Publishing
A division of Pioneer Drama Service, Inc.
PO Box 4267
Englewood, CO 80155

www.pioneerdrama.com

Editor: Nicole Deemes
Cover design: Devin Watson
Project manager: Karen Bullock

Library of Congress Cataloging-in-Publication Data

Ewen, Jan Peterson.
    Sci-fi scenes and monster dreams: 16 comedy scenes for student   actors / Jan Peterson Ewen. – First edition.
        pages cm
Includes bibliographical references.
ISBN 978-1-56608-197-9 (pbk. : alk. paper)
1. Young adult drama, American. 2. Teenagers—Drama. I. Title.
PS3601.W45E94 2015
792.9'5–dc23
                                    2015023393

1   2   3   15   16   17

To my wonderful family —
Bruce, Peter, Rebecca, and Rachel.

To my brother, John, who first suggested
I write science fiction scenes for student actors.

And to all my acting students who inspire
outrageous creativity!

1. Table of Contents

1. You Complete Me

RUNNING TIME: 9 minutes

CAST SIZE: 1M, 5E

CAST OF CHARACTERS

DR. MADD .... eccentric, egotistical scientist
I. GORE .... Dr. Madd's hunch-backed
assistant
MR. WINKOWSKI .... head that has been preserved
by cryonics for thirty years
BODY #1 .... former bodybuilder
BODY #2 .... former ballet dancer
BODY #3 .... former couch potato

SETTING

Dr. Madd's laboratory.

PROPERTIES

Large box, cloth, table, beakers, surgical utensils, humorous "mad scientist" items, functioning hair dryer, tray with more surgical utensils, stopwatch, bathrobe, bag of chips, rubber gloves.

OPTIONAL LIGHTING

Blue spotlight.

You Complete Me

· · · · · · ·

There is a large box at CENTER upon which "sits" the head of MR. WINKOWSKI. The body of the actor is inside the box so it cannot be seen. At the beginning of the scene, the head is covered with a cloth. A table sits nearby, covered with beakers, surgical utensils, humorous "mad scientist" props, and a hair dryer. DR. MADD ENTERS RIGHT, carrying a stopwatch and rubber gloves in a pocket, and addresses the AUDIENCE in a serious and slightly maniacal manner. I. GORE ENTERS RIGHT behind DR. MADD, carrying a tray of surgical utensils, which he places on the box beside the covered head as DR. MADD addresses the AUDIENCE.

DR. MADD: *(Slowly and with reverence.)* Ladies and gentlemen, my esteemed colleagues, and members of the press, thank you for coming to my laboratory this evening. What you are about to see will no doubt shock you and challenge everything you have ever assumed about the preservation of the body and the controversial field of cryonics. It is my great privilege to share with you tonight a breakthrough of universal proportions. *(Becomes increasingly agitated.)* You will be the first humans ever to observe the successful reattachment of a cryopreserved head to a cryopreserved body and the reanimation of a human being who has existed in a state of neuro-suspension for over thirty years. Yes, ladies and gentlemen, it is now possible to do the impossible, and I, Dr. Madd... *(Emits an evil laugh.)* ... have discovered the elusive scientific process all on my own, with no help from any of the rest of the scientific community, which has ridiculed me in the past! *(Regains composure.)* Now, let us begin with a brief introduction. *(Motions to I. GORE.)* This is my faithful assistant, I. Gore. Say hello to the nice people, I. Gore.

2

I. GORE: *(Waves to the AUDIENCE.)* Hello, nice people.

DR. MADD: *(Crosses to the box.)* Excellent. And now, I. Gore, will you please do the honors? *(I. GORE moves to the box and quickly lifts the cloth from the head to reveal MR. WINKOWSKI, whose eyes are closed.)* This, ladies and gentlemen, is the head of Mr. Darryl Winkowski, a former citizen of the little town of Walla Walla, Washington. Mr. Winkowski worked as a plumber for thirty-six long years until that fateful day when he was accidentally electrocuted while standing in a puddle beneath a broken water pipe. As per his instructions, he was rushed to our laboratory where we immediately saved his head, placed it in a metal tank filled with liquid nitrogen, and reduced the temperature to minus three hundred and twenty degrees Fahrenheit. That is where Mr. Darryl Winkowski—in a state of complete neuro-suspension—has existed for the past thirty years, waiting, just waiting, for the day when I would discover the technology that would give him an incredible new life! *(Emits evil laugh.)* And now, with the help of my faithful assistant, I will bring Mr. Winkowski's head back up to room temperature. *(Dramatic.)* This is a crucial part of the procedure. If the warming isn't done at exactly the right speed and exactly the right temperature, the cells could form ice crystals and shatter. And I'm sure you can imagine what a mess that would be. Are you ready, I. Gore?

I. GORE: *(Holds up the hair dryer.)* Ready, Doctor.

DR. MADD: *(Serious.)* Begin the thawing process. *(I. GORE begins to blow-dry MR. WINKOWSKI on high speed. DR. MADD pulls a stopwatch from his pocket, pushes the button, and begins to time the thaw.)* Ten, nine, eight, seven, six, five, four, three, two, and one. Stop! Not a microsecond more!

I. GORE: *(Quickly shuts off hair dryer as DR. MADD crosses to the box and puts the back of a hand on MR. WINKOWSKI'S forehead.)* What do you think, Dr. Madd?

DR. MADD: It's perfect! Ninety-eight point six degrees exactly! Good work, I. Gore.

I. GORE: Thank you, Doctor.

MR. WINKOWSKI: *(Moans, blinks his eyes, yawns a big yawn, and broadly stretches his facial muscles.)* What's going on? Where am I? *(Tries to look around, but his head cannot move in either direction.)* Who are you?

DR. MADD: I, Mr. Winkowski, am the famous Dr. Madd, head scientist and researcher of the Madd Cryonics Corporation, LLC, and you, Mr. Winkowski, have been successfully reanimated! *(Emits an evil laugh. I. GORE tries to imitate it but receives a stern look from DR. MADD.)*

MR. WINKOWSKI: What? No kidding? It worked? The cryonic thing worked? I'm alive?

DR. MADD: Yes, you are alive—thanks to me!

MR. WINKOWSKI: *(Amazed.)* Well, I'll be! I'm alive! I'm alive! I'm... *(Realizes he has no body and begins to panic.)* Hey, wait a minute! Where's the rest of me? Where's my body? Where are my legs? What's going on?

DR. MADD: Don't worry, Mr. Winkowski. Everything's fine. Thirty years ago, when you were frozen, we only had the technology to save your head. But now, thanks to highly advanced nanotechnology, I have developed a way to manipulate matter on the cellular level, making it possible to reattach your head to the body of another victim—I mean, *person*—thereby creating a super-human with your head and the body of your choosing.

MR. WINKOWSKI: The body of my choosing? What are you talking about? I don't want a new body! I want my old body!

DR. MADD: Ah! But wait until you see the bodies I have lined up for you, Mr. Winkowski. I. Gore, prepare the bodies!

I. GORE: Yes, Doctor! *(EXITS LEFT.)*

DR. MADD: Mr. Winkowski, now you will view an assortment of forms presented as holograms. Each form is still sporting its former master's noggin, so you'll have to use a little imagination as to what the body will look like with your skull attached. Mind you, these are premium quality bodies, each one in excellent physical condition—more or less—at the time they were frozen.

MR. WINKOWSKI: I suppose it can't hurt to take a look.

DR. MADD: *(With flourish.)* Excellent! I. Gore, present the first hologram, please.

I. GORE: *(ENTERS LEFT.)* Yes, Dr. Madd. Presenting the first spectacular body. *(BODY #1 ENTERS LEFT, strikes a bodybuilder's pose, and continues to strike new poses. [NOTE: If you have access to spotlights, put the actor in a blue light to suggest that this is a hologram.])*

DR. MADD: *(As if hosting a game show.)* For your consideration, the exquisite physique of an award-winning former bodybuilder. Fulfill your dream of being a world-class athlete and live in peak physical condition from this day forward. This body comes to you with no more than three percent body fat, ridiculously broad shoulders, bulging triceps, and a resting heart rate of fifty-five beats per minute. Amazing! And this body can be all yours. Just say the word and I will attach you!

I. GORE: It's a beauty!

MR. WINKOWSKI: *(Considers carefully.)* Well, I don't know. It's obviously a good body and all, but it looks like it would take an awful lot of upkeep. I really hate working out and going to the gym. Don't you have something a little easier to maintain?

DR. MADD: *(Surprised.)* Of course. Perhaps our second body will be more to your liking. I. Gore, bring out the next body, please.

I. GORE: Yes, Dr. Madd. *(BODY #1 EXITS LEFT as BODY #2 ENTERS LEFT. It runs onto the stage, strikes a ballet pose* *and continues to dance and strike poses.)* Presenting the second magnificent body!

DR. MADD: Ah, yes! Here we have something a little more on the "artsy" side. In this amazing new body, you will experience grace and agility, flying through the air as you tour jetè, leaping and turning. Pirouette! Chassé! Cabriole! The crowd will cheer and throw flowers at your lovely feet!

I. GORE: *(Claps hands.)* Bravo! Bravo! *(If BODY #2 is female, I. GORE should say "Brava" instead.)*

MR. WINKOWSKI: Stop! Stop! I'm getting dizzy! No, no. Too much work! Look. I'm sorry, but I don't want to be a bodybuilder or a ballet dancer. I just want to live a simple life with a body that can take me from one place to another without breaking down every five minutes. Do you have anything like that?

DR. MADD: *(Disappointed.)* Of course, Mr. Winkowski. I was saving the best for last. I. Gore, bring in the third and final hologram, please.

I. GORE: *(With little enthusiasm.)* Yes, Doctor. *(BODY #2 EXITS LEFT as BODY #3 ENTERS LEFT, stands limply, and looks from side to side without exhibiting the least amount of energy. It wears an old bathrobe and carries a bag of chips that it snacks on.)* Presenting body number three.

DR. MADD: I must warn you, Mr. Winkowski, body number three lived its life as little more than a couch potato. It had no particular interests or ambitions. It watched a lot of television, played video games for hours on end, and ate nothing but junk food. I don't think this is necessarily the best—

MR. WINKOWSKI: *(Interrupts, excited.)* It's perfect! I love it! So it's a bit of a fixer-upper, but I enjoy a good project. I'll take it!

DR. MADD: But Mr. Winkowski, are you sure?

MR. WINKOWSKI: Yes, I'm sure! I want that one, warts and all.

DR. MADD: Very well. As you wish. I. Gore, prepare body number three for the experiment! *(Stops suddenly and corrects.)* I mean, the *surgery*.

I. GORE: I'll thaw it out immediately, Doctor. *(EXITS LEFT with BODY #3.)*

MR. WINKOWSKI: Oh, boy! I can hardly wait! I'm going to get my life back! Whoopee! So how long is this surgery going to take, Doc?

DR. MADD: *(Puts on a pair of rubber gloves.)* I'm not exactly sure.

MR. WINKOWSKI: You're not? How long did the last reattachment take?

DR. MADD: Only about thirty minutes. But then again, it was on a mouse. Very small neck, you see.

MR. WINKOWSKI: What?! A mouse? Wait a minute! Have you ever done this procedure on a human before?

DR. MADD: Not exactly. But it worked great on the mouse.

MR. WINKOWSKI: It worked great on the mouse?

DR. MADD: *(Stops and considers.)* Well, pretty great. Not too bad actually. *(Sums up.)* Pretty, almost, not too bad.

MR. WINKOWSKI: "Pretty, almost, not too bad?" That sounds terrible!

DR. MADD: No, it wasn't *terrible*. Not *quite* terrible. It was very, not quite terrible. In fact, it was almost promising. A few minor adjustments, and we'll be just fine.

I. GORE: *(ENTERS LEFT.)* Body number three is ready for the experiment—I mean, the *surgery*, Doctor.

DR. MADD: Excellent! Let's begin.

MR. WINKOWSKI: *(Emphatic.)* No, no wait! Hold on! I changed my mind. I don't want the surgery. I want to be frozen again! Just put me back in the deep freeze until you've worked out all the bugs. Help! Someone! *(DR. MADD walks to the box and puts both hands on MR. WINKOWSKI'S head as if to pick it up.)* Really, I just want to wait a few more years before I'm reattached. I'm still pretty sleepy. *(Fakes a big yawn.)*

DR. MADD: Don't worry, Mr. Winkowski. This will all be over in no time, and you'll be a new man with a new body! Ready? *(To AUDIENCE.)* We'll be right back, folks. Right this way, Mr. Winkowski! *(Pretends to lift the head as MR. WINKOWSKI screams.)*

MR. WINKOWSKI: Help!

· · · · · · ·

2. How Time Flies

RUNNING TIME: 10 minutes

CAST SIZE: 2M, 3E

CAST OF CHARACTERS

TRAVELER #1..................inventor of a time machine

TRAVELER #2..................investor behind the time travel experiment

TRAVELER #3..................biologist and doubting participant

GEORGY-BOY..................Captain Blimey's right-hand man

CAPTAIN BLIMEY ....nasty, old pirate captain

SETTING

TIME: The year 1700.

PLACE: The countryside near a seashore.

PROPERTIES

Mechanism to represent a hand-held time machine, fancy shoulder bag, aviator sunglasses, notebook, pen, three cellphones, earphones, eye patch, two swords.

How Time Flies

· · · · · · ·

The three TRAVELERS throw themselves ON LEFT. TRAVELER #1 holds a mechanism in both hands that represents the time machine controller. TRAVELER #2 is wearing expensive-looking clothes, aviator sunglasses, and a fancy shoulder bag. TRAVELER #3 carries a notebook and pen.

TRAVELER #2: *(Stumbles, breathless.)* Where are we? Where are we?

TRAVELER #1: *(Amazed.)* It worked! Oh, my gosh! It really worked! I knew it would! My time machine worked!

TRAVELER #2: It worked! We'll be rich! Well, you'll be rich. I'll be richer.

TRAVELER #3: *(Less enthusiastic.)* We don't actually know if it worked. We could be anywhere.

TRAVELER #1: Everybody, check to see if you're all here. *(The three TRAVELERS pat themselves down from head to foot.)*

TRAVELER #2: I'm all here.

TRAVELER #1: I'm all here.

TRAVELER #3: Confirmed. Recombination of particles appears to be successful. *(Writes a note.)*

TRAVELER #2: But we have no idea where we are!

TRAVELER #1: *(Excited.)* We're somewhere, and it's not where we started, so the time machine must have worked! That's what's important. We have been transported to another time and another place thanks to this brilliant invention of mine. *(Kisses the time travel mechanism.)*

TRAVELER #3: Maybe we should hold off on the celebrating until we figure out where we are and *when* we are. Did you set that thing for a specific year? Is it possible that we have simply been reassembled in a different place but not actually in a different time?

TRAVELER #1: Of course I set it to a specific year. I am an award-winning physicist, for heaven's sake! I thought we'd test it out with a time period that wasn't too challenging, just a little leap into the past, you know. Nothing extravagant. I set it for the year 1700.

TRAVELER #2: Why did you choose the year 1700?

TRAVELER #1: Because it is significantly different from our own time, so we will have no trouble identifying the time period for our research. Just think! In 1700, people existed without complicated machines, without state-of-the-art computers, and without nanotechnology! Fascinating! And besides, I like even, round numbers.

TRAVELER #3: You like even, round numbers? Sheesh! Some award-winning physicist you are.

TRAVELER #2: *(Takes sunglasses off and puts them on his/ her head.)* I may be just the money behind this project, but I am ready to get down to some serious scientific research. How are we going to know if we're in the year 1700? What are we looking for? There are no signs of life around here. We may have dropped into the middle of nowhere! *(Looks out toward the AUDIENCE.)* Here we are on the shore of some vast sea or ocean, no houses around, no people, no vehicles, and no super malls. What do we do?

TRAVELER #1: We start looking for clues. Telltale signs that will prove we have been transported back to the year 1700.

TRAVELER #3: Like what?

TRAVELER #1: I don't know! You're a biologist. Take some plant samples! Identify something unusual! I'm sure you will recognize proof when you see it. Now I suggest we split up and explore the area then meet back here at these precise coordinates to compare our results. Check coordinates. *(The TRAVELERS each take out a small, cell-phone-sized personal computer. TRAVELER #1 and TRAVELER #3 punch a few buttons then return them to their pockets. TRAVELER #2 connects earphones and starts rocking out to music only he/she can hear then notices that the OTHERS are scowling.)*

TRAVELER #2: What? I need a little music for the road.

TRAVELER #3: You won't be able to hear us if you're wearing those things.

TRAVELER #2: *(Takes off the earphones.)* Okay, okay. Man, science is no fun at all.

TRAVELER #1: I think we're ready to branch out. I don't think we should get too far away from each other.

TRAVELER #3: I agree. Let's stay within shouting range.

TRAVELER #1: All right. *(Points OFF UP RIGHT.)* You head west, and you head north. I'll explore to the south. *(Walks slowly DOWN CENTER, examining the area carefully. TRAVELER #3 explores UP LEFT as TRAVELER #2 EXITS RIGHT.)*

TRAVELER #2: *(From OFF RIGHT.)* I think I found the proof we need.

TRAVELER #1: *(To TRAVELER #3.)* We've found something already! Come on! *(Waves TRAVELER #3 to follow and runs STAGE RIGHT. TRAVELER #2 ENTERS RIGHT with hands raised in the air, followed by CAPTAIN BLIMEY and GEORGY-BOY, who wears an eye patch over his right eye. They each have a sword and point them at TRAVELER #2'S back.)*

TRAVELER #2: *(To TRAVELERS.)* Is this sufficient proof for you? *(TRAVELER #1 and TRAVELER #3 raise their hands in the air as well and walk backward toward CENTER.)*

GEORGY-BOY: Looky here, Cap'n. There's two more of 'em!

CAPTAIN BLIMEY: You're right, Georgy-Boy. But the question is, what *are* they? *(Walks around the*

TRAVELERS, holding them at bay with his sword.) They don't look like any jack tars I've ever seen. By the way they're dressed, I'd say they might be some of them Frenchies.

GEORGY-BOY: They look like a bunch o' landlubbers, don't they, Cap'n? *(Laughs and mocks the TRAVELERS.)* All dressed up in their fancy clothes. La-dee-da! I ain't seen nothin' like it before!

CAPTAIN BLIMEY: They're foreigners, all right. Keep a close eye on them, Georgy-Boy. They look like a slippery lot, they do.

GEORGY-BOY: *(Grins.)* Don't worry, Cap'n. Me and ol' Slicer, here *(Indicates his sword.)*, is keepin' a real close eye on them. *(Switches eye patch from the right eye to the left eye.)*

CAPTAIN BLIMEY: Hand over your treasure! Gold, coins, doubloons, jewels—everything you have, and make it quick. *(Admires TRAVELER #2'S shoulder bag.)* I'll take that little purse of yours, matey.

TRAVELER #2: I beg your pardon! This is not a purse! This is a fine European shoulder bag.

CAPTAIN BLIMEY: Looks like a lassie purse to me. Hand it over! *(TRAVELER #2 reluctantly hands over the bag.)*

GEORGY-BOY: *(Takes sunglasses off TRAVELER #2'S head.)* Looky here, Cap'n. This one's got two eye patches! How can he see with two eye patches on? *(Holds sunglasses up to his eyes.)* Blimey! You can see right through 'em! What kind of black magic is this?

TRAVELER #2: *(Grabs the sunglasses back.)* Watch out, you buffoon! That's my favorite pair of aviators!

TRAVELER #1: Excuse me, Captain, is it? *(Extends a hand to shake.)* Allow me to introduce myself and my fellow colleagues. *(Lowers hand when CAPTAIN BLIMEY does not shake.)* We are scientists from the United States of America, and we are conducting a trial of my new time travel machine—which is a brilliant invention, if I do say so myself. It has enabled us to visit this time and place and learn about your colorful way of life. *(Shows them the mechanism. CAPTAIN BLIMEY and GEORGY-BOY shrink back.)*

GEORGY-BOY: *(Frightened.)* What is it, Cap'n?

CAPTAIN BLIMEY: *(Cautious.)* Some sort of mysterious box, Georgy-Boy. Stay back, and don't let these strangers out of your sight for a minute!

TRAVELER #3: You see, we were aiming for the year 1700, primarily because the inventor likes even numbers. Can you tell us whether we have reached the right century? *(CAPTAIN BLIMEY and GEORGY-BOY look very confused.)*

TRAVELER #2: What we're trying to ask is—what year is it?

CAPTAIN BLIMEY: What sort of witchcraft is this? You certainly aren't from around here. You dress in strange clothing and you don't even know what year it is?

GEORGY-BOY: Careful, Cap'n. They be a strange bunch. Maybe they've been drinkin' a bit too much from the ol' bottle o' rum. Know what I mean?

CAPTAIN BLIMEY: No matter. They'll make strong servants, drunk or sober. Let's take them aboard and put them to work. There's many a deck to be swabbed. Give me that magic box. I'm going to send it to the bottom of the seven seas where it belongs. *(PIRATES start to push the TRAVELERS OFF RIGHT.)*

TRAVELER #1: *(Clutches the mechanism.)* Wait just a minute! We aren't going anywhere with you. And you are absolutely not getting my time machine.

TRAVELER #2: That's right! And we're definitely not going to swab your decks! These are three-hundred-dollar shoes I have on!

TRAVELER #3: We are noted scientists, and we are in the middle of conducting a groundbreaking experiment. So if you don't mind, just tell us what year this is, and we'll be on our way.

GEORGY-BOY: *(Brief pause, then the PIRATES burst out laughing.)* I must admit, they got a lot of spunk for worthless ol' prisoners.

CAPTAIN BLIMEY: They certainly do. Perhaps they don't exactly understand the King's English. Let me make the situation clearer to them. *(Talks slowly.)* You are now our prisoners. Your magic box and all your riches belong to me. *(Takes the sunglasses back from TRAVELER #2.)* We are taking you back to our ship where you can either swab the decks or walk the plank. The choice is yours. Do you understand me now?

TRAVELER #2: *(Aside to the OTHER TRAVELERS.)* Um, I don't think this is going exactly as planned.

TRAVELER #3: Agreed. I think we need to come up with an alternative course of action as quickly as possible. Perhaps select a different year on that brilliant machine of yours, and bid the cutthroats *arrivederci*!

TRAVELER #2: I concur. Select a different year, and zap us out of here now!

TRAVELER #1: *(Pushes buttons rapidly on the time travel mechanism.)* I'm on it. Just give me a couple of moments to work my magic. We should just go back to our own century and leave well enough alone. Okay, that should do it. Stay close, everybody. *(TRAVELERS huddle together and inch away from the PIRATES.)* That's better. One, two—

TRAVELER #3: *(Interrupts.)* Wait! We still need some proof. If we don't have something concrete, nobody will believe we've been here.

GEORGY-BOY: What's the holdup, here? Let's get moving!

TRAVELER #1: *(To PIRATES.)* We'll be with you in a moment. *(Turns back and whispers loudly to the OTHERS.)* We have to get out of here. There's no time to waste. They want to turn us into swabbing swashbucklers!

TRAVELER #3: I've got an idea. Start counting slowly!

TRAVELER #1: *(Starts counting again.)* One... two...

TRAVELER #3: *(Runs to GEORGY-BOY and points into the AUDIENCE.)* Hey, Georgy-Boy, look! It's a sea monster!

GEORGY-BOY: *(Looks out where TRAVELER #3 points.)* Nessie? Where? Where? *(TRAVELER #3 grabs GEORGY-BOY'S sword and returns to the huddle. TRAVELER #2 runs to CAPTAIN BLIMEY, grabs the sunglasses, then runs back to the huddle just as TRAVELER #1 finishes.)*

TRAVELER #1: ...three! *(TRAVELERS run OFF LEFT. CAPTAIN BLIMEY and GEORGY-BOY look around in fear and amazement.)*

GEORGY-BOY: Where did they go? The eye patch is gone! And me sword! What happened to me sword?

CAPTAIN BLIMEY: They disappeared! Just like that. Poof! And they took ol' Slicer with them.

GEORGY-BOY: *(Despairs.)* No! Not ol' Slicer! He was me favorite weapon of all time. I may never fight again! *(Shifts to anger and fear.)* It's witchcraft, I tell you. Witchcraft!

CAPTAIN BLIMEY: You may be right, Georgy-Boy. This place must be haunted. Let's get back to the ship before those demons decide to return. And whatever you do, don't mention what happened here to anyone! You hear me?

GEORGY-BOY: *(Salutes.)* Aye-aye, Cap'n. You can count on me. Me lips is sealed. *(Pantomimes locking his lips and throwing away the key.)* No one will be callin' us daft!

CAPTAIN BLIMEY: Good. Let's go ransack a village or two. That'll lift our spirits. *(Runs OFF RIGHT)*

GEORGY-BOY: *(Lingers behind and looks around warily. To himself.)* Witchcraft. That's what it is. Nothin' but witchcraft. *(Runs OFF RIGHT, crying out in anguish.)* Slicer!

· · · · · · ·

3. BUNK MATES

RUNNING TIME: 5 minutes

CAST SIZE: 2E

CAST OF CHARACTERS

JESSE/JESSI ....avid reader with a big
imagination
MONSTER.......................friendly monster; lives under
Jesse's bed

SETTING

Jesse's bedroom.

PROPERTIES

Sturdy table or bench, sheet, pillow, flashlight, book, plate of cookies, glass of milk.

Bunk Mates

·······

JESSE sits on a sturdy table or bench used as a bed at CENTER with a sheet over his head. He has a pillow, a working flashlight, and a book under the sheet and is reading the end of a scary story out loud to himself.

JESSE: *(Reads slowly.)* "So the boy gathered all his courage and slowly looked under his bed. There it was, just as he had feared—a huge, disgusting, hairy monster, with glistening fangs and sharp, yellow claws the size of butcher knives. The beast stared at the boy with his dark, black eyes. Saliva dripped from his fangs. Suddenly, the creature pounced. And the boy was never heard from again. The end." *(Closes the book, turns off the flashlight, and sticks his face out, leaving the sheet over his head for protection. He nervously looks around the bedroom, then slowly peeks under his bed.)*

MONSTER: *(ENTERS RIGHT with a plate of cookies and a glass of milk and watches for a moment.)* Did I miss the ending? *(JESSE turns to see MONSTER and screams. Then MONSTER screams. Then JESSE screams. Then MONSTER screams again.)* Whoa, whoa! What are we screaming about? What happened?

JESSE: *(Terrified, crouches on the bed and points at MONSTER.)* You're... You're...

MONSTER: I'm... I'm... what? Too late to hear the end of the story? Did the boy find the monster, or was it just his imagination? *(Settles down under JESSE'S bed.)*

JESSE: You're... You're...

MONSTER: Could you please read that last part again? I knew I should have waited to get a snack, but I was just so hungry. I think I left at the part where there was a huge storm with thunder and lightning. Go ahead. Start there. *(Eats a cookie.)*

JESSE: You're... You're a monster!

MONSTER: You don't have to sound so disgusted about it, Jesse. I do have feelings, you know. We have never been properly introduced. My name is Mel. *(Holds out a hand to shake, but JESSE keeps his hands tucked into his chest, so MONSTER pulls the hand back.)* Suit yourself. Would you like a cookie?

JESSE: What are you doing under my bed?

MONSTER: Is that a trick question? What does it look like I'm doing under your bed? I'm listening to you read a book. And by the way, I really like this one. It's a thriller! Read the ending again. *(Begs sweetly.)* Please.

JESSE: *(Gains some courage.)* Get out! Get out of my bedroom!

MONSTER: What are you talking about, Jesse? This is my home. I live here. I'm not going anywhere. Now stop with the hysterics and read that ending!

JESSE: *(Still nervous, gets down from his bed holding his pillow and walks around to face the MONSTER.)* Look here, monster. I don't know who you are or where you came from, but I want you out from under my bed this instant, or I'll have to pummel you with my pillow.

MONSTER: A pillow fight? That sounds like fun. Right after we finish the story.

JESSE: *(Frustrated.)* Oooh! You're not hearing me! Pack it up! Hit the road! Clear out, buddy! *(MONSTER continues eating and ignores JESSE'S demands.)* How long have you lived under there, anyway?

MONSTER: Let's see, you got this bed about five years ago, and I came with the bed, so I'd say... *(Calculates on five fingers.)* ...I've lived under here for about five years.

JESSE: *(Shocked.)* Five years? You've lived under my bed for five years and I never knew it? That can't be true!

MONSTER: Why not? Just because you've never paid any attention to me before?

JESSE: But I would have seen you, or heard you, or—

MONSTER: Oh, you knew I was here. You just didn't want to admit it. Look, Jesse—who do you think put that dollar under your pillow when you lost your first tooth? Some fairy? No way, José. That was me! And who retrieved all the library books you dropped down here? Me, that's who. I scooted them out so you could see them. I saved you a fortune in overdue fines. And have you ever worried about burglars or bad guys breaking into this house?

JESSE: *(Thinks.)* No, not really.

MONSTER: Of course not! Because you knew in your heart of hearts that I was down here watching out for you and listening to you read your stories. Besides, you have seen me a few times.

JESSE: I have? *(Thinks.)* That's right! I have! I thought you looked familiar. But that was just a nightmare.

MONSTER: No, that was me. I was getting my midnight milk and cookies. I love your mother's cookies. My favorite are the snickerdoodles. I tried to tiptoe, but you still heard me. It's not easy for a monster to tiptoe, you know.

JESSE: But what if I don't want a monster living under my bed?

MONSTER: Why not? I don't see any downside to the situation. I watch over you while you sleep peacefully. You love to read stories out loud. I love to listen to the stories you read. I even put up with you using our bed as a trampoline from time to time. Do you have any idea how annoying that is? I think that's very generous of me.

JESSE: I don't know about this. I guess it doesn't really hurt to have you live under there. As long as you don't pounce on me in the night.

MONSTER: Pounce on you? Why would I want to do a thing like that? Too strenuous. As long as you keep the milk and cookies coming, I'll be a happy camper. By the way, you might want to mention to your mom that we're out of snickerdoodles. Now get back to that story! I want to hear what happens to that boy in the end. *(Settles in to listen.)*

JESSE: *(Uncertain, pulls the sheet over his head, turns on the flashlight, and opens the book.)* "So, the boy gathered all his courage and slowly looked under his bed." *(Pokes his head out and finishes the story differently.)* And they all lived happily ever after. The end. *(Slams the book closed and ducks under his sheet.)* Good night, Mel.

MONSTER: *(Sighs with delight.)* Ah! What a perfect ending. I couldn't have written it better myself. Good night, Jesse.

· · · · · · ·

4. You Don't Say

RUNNING TIME: 10 minutes

CAST SIZE: 2M, 2F, 1E

CAST OF CHARACTERS

KAYE NYNE .... manager of the dog shelter
PETE .... kindhearted person looking for
a canine companion
ROOSEVELT .... sociable and sweet-tempered
American Bulldog
APHRODITE.................... gorgeous and smart French
Poodle
NELSON .... motley but practical mutt

SETTING

The back room of a shelter for dogs.

PROPERTIES

Three large boxes, stool or chair, three signs that read: "Aphrodite, French Poodle, 5 years old"; "Roosevelt, American Bulldog, 4 years old"; and "Nelson, Mixed Breed, age unknown."

You Don't Say

· · · · · · ·

The room has three large boxes used as kennels at CENTER, each containing a dog who is waiting to be adopted. There is a sign on each cage describing the animal inside. There is a stool or chair near the cages. The DOGS are all curled up, sleeping in their separate kennels as KAYE NYNE and PETE ENTER LEFT.

KAYE NYNE: Here they are. These three dogs have been here for several weeks now. We can only house them for a few more days, then we'll have to—well, you know.

PETE: Oh, man. That's terrible. Hopefully I can take one of them home with me today.

KAYE NYNE: That would be great, but you need to make sure you choose the right dog to fit your lifestyle or they will just end up back in the shelter again. So take your time and find just the right match for you. They've all had their shots, and they're ready to go. You can open the cages and meet them if you like. *(Notices PETE looking uncertain and reassures him.)* Don't worry. They won't bite. I'll be right out front when you're finished. I'm just going to leave you alone so you can get to know them.

PETE: *(Nervous.)* Okay. Are you sure they won't mind having a stranger approach them?

KAYE NYNE: Heavens, no. They're very sociable and used to having people around. They meet new people every day.

PETE: *(Calms down a bit.)* Oh. Okay. I'm really excited about this. I live in a big house all by myself, and I have several acres of property for a dog to run around and explore. *(DOGS perk up at this description.)*

KAYE NYNE: It sounds like you have the perfect home for these animals. Take your time, now. Get to know them real well. They all have different personalities, as you will see. Find the one that's right for you. *(EXITS LEFT.)*

PETE: *(Starts to look into the cages.)* Let's see who we have here. This cage says "Aphrodite," and you are a French Poodle, five years old. Hello, Aphrodite. My name is Pete. My, you're pretty, aren't you? *(APHRODITE strikes a pose and pants happily. PETE reaches in the kennel and pats her head, then moves down the row of cages. Reads the next sign.)* And you are Roosevelt. That's a funny name for a bulldog. Roosevelt... Bully! Bully! *(ROOSEVELT rolls his eyes as if he's heard this many times before.)* It says here that you're four years old. Hi there, Roosevelt. You look like a happy little guy. *(ROOSEVELT smiles and pants as PETE scratches him on the head. PETE moves down the row to the third cage.)* And who do we have here? *(Reads the sign.)* It says here that your name is Nelson, and you are a mixed breed.

APHRODITE: That's the politically correct way of saying he's a mutt.

PETE: *(Startled, jumps and turns but sees no one.)* Oh! I thought I heard someone come in. *(Calms down.)* It must have been my imagination.

NELSON: I wish she was in your imagination. *(Calls to APHRODITE.)* Hey, Aphrodite, mind your own business, why don't you! I'm talking with the nice man, here.

PETE: *(Jumps again and looks at NELSON in shock.)* Did you... did you... just say something?

ROOSEVELT: Hey, buddy! Don't pay any attention to those two. I'm the only one with any manners around here. Now let's talk adoption.

PETE: *(Jumps a third time and starts to panic.)* What's going on here? I must be hallucinating! I'm hearing things that aren't real! What did I have for lunch today?

Maybe I have food poisoning. *(Paces back and forth.)* I have to get out of here.

APHRODITE: Here we go again.

NELSON: Another nervous Nellie.

ROOSEVELT: Hey, buddy! Calm down, will you? You're going to arouse suspicion.

APHRODITE: We're not going to hurt you. We just want to communicate a little, that's all.

PETE: *(Stops pacing and looks at the DOGS.)* Dogs cannot talk! You are not supposed to talk! This can't be happening! I must be losing my mind.

ROOSEVELT: Why do humans think it's such a big deal that dogs can talk? We've been listening to you all rattle on for centuries! You don't think we might have picked up a small vocabulary over the years? Sheesh!

APHRODITE: It's insulting, that's what it is! Humans think they're so superior to other creatures.

NELSON: Yeah! Like it takes some real genius to put a few words together. Give me a break.

PETE: I can't believe this. How long have you been able to talk?

NELSON: I don't know. All my life, I guess.

APHRODITE: Of course, not all dogs talk. Some don't even try. They're happy just getting the occasional pat on the head and playing dumb. It's insulting to the rest of us, really.

PETE: No, no. This can't be happening. I've got to get out of here. *(Starts LEFT.)*

ROOSEVELT: Hey, get back here! We're not done talking to you yet. Open these cages so we can have a real conversation.

PETE: I'm not going to open your cages! For all I know, you'll attack me or try to escape or something like that! *(DOGS laugh hysterically.)*

APHRODITE: Oh, don't be ridiculous!

ROOSEVELT: What do you think we are? A pack of wolves? Come on. Let us out of here!

NELSON: We just want to discuss this whole adoption thing in a calm, rational way. Come on. We're not going to hurt you. *(DOGS give PETE very innocent, pleading looks.)*

PETE: *(Hesitant.)* Are you telling me the truth? You promise you won't hurt me if I let you out?

ALL DOGS: We promise!

PETE: *(Inches toward the cages.)* No funny stuff?

ALL DOGS: No funny stuff.

PETE: It's against my better judgment, but I'll let you out. Apparently I'm cracking up anyway, and none of this is really happening, so what have I got to lose? I'll just let the talking dogs out of their cages and have a conversation with them. Why not? Happens every day! *(Opens each cage then steps back, unsure. DOGS come out, stretch, and move freely.)*

NELSON: This is fantastic! Freedom! Beautiful freedom! The wide open spaces!

APHRODITE: Ugh! I was feeling so cramped in there. I just couldn't bear it another minute.

ROOSEVELT: *(Pulls up a stool, and PETE sits down.)* Let's get down to business. *(OTHER DOGS crowd around the stool.)* You're looking for a dog. We're looking for a home. We don't have much time left.

APHRODITE: Oh! I feel faint.

NELSON: Hold it together, Aphrodite. Your fainting is not going to get us out of this joint. This guy here's our only hope.

ROOSEVELT: That's right. That's why we're talking to you right now. We're desperate. You've got to hear us out. I am a purebred bulldog. I am sociable and sweet-tempered, but don't let my adorable exterior fool you.

I am also a vicious guard dog with a reputation for courage. Though, I am at heart a lover not a fighter. I may not be overly lively, but I am dignified, and I will admit, occasionally I can be a bit stubborn. I am very easygoing. We can just kick back together, take a nap in the afternoon, and maybe go for a little stroll. I won't be a bother, and I will only speak when spoken to, if that is your preference. In other words, the perfect companion.

PETE: Well, Roosevelt, that sounds pretty good. You do sound like you would make an excellent companion.

APHRODITE: Now, hold on, hold on. Roosevelt neglected to tell you that he also snorts a lot, and I'm pretty sure he has sleep apnea. He would be fine for a lazy couch-potato kind of guy, but it's obvious that you are the active, adventurous sort, Pete. *(Flirtatious.)* You work out, don't you?

PETE: *(Flattered.)* I do try to keep in shape.

APHRODITE: Exactly! You spend a few years on the couch with Roosevelt and those six-pack abs of yours will be a distant memory! Now I, on the other hand, am a purebred poodle. I'm gorgeous, aren't I? Admit it! But not only am I beautiful, I'm also strong and athletic. Wouldn't we look good walking down the street together? *(Prances around a little.)*

PETE: I guess…

APHRODITE: I am known for being sophisticated and smart. *(Leans in to PETE and winks.)* These other two are pretty low on the old IQ chart, if you catch my drift. *(Straightens up.)* I am at the top of the curve when it comes to smarts. Just think of the conversations we could have discussing the day's events, watching CNN, and listening to NPR. How glorious! *(Grabs PETE'S hand.)* Come on. Let's go home!

NELSON: Wait just one little minute there, sister. It's my turn to plead my case. I may not be some fancy purebred like Aphrodite and Roosevelt, here, but I got a great mix of genes in me. It sounds like what you need at that big old place of yours is some major security. Well, guess what? I am part German Shepherd, which makes me an excellent guard dog, but I've also got a little Labrador in the mix, which makes me as faithful as a canine companion can get. And that's not all. I also have a smidgeon of dachshund so I can still fit on your lap when you need a little snuggle time. Why settle for just one breed when you can get the perfect mix! *(ALL DOGS start talking at once, ad-libbing their cases.)*

PETE: *(Overwhelmed.)* Okay, okay. Just stop! Stop! *(Stands and starts to pace again.)* This is too much! It's insane! Talking dogs? I'm having a hard time believing all this! For all I know, you may be from another planet or something like that! Some planet where all the dogs walk around talking and the people just sit there barking and scratching themselves. Maybe I just better lock you up again and get the heck out of here!

ALL DOGS: *(Plead, ad-libbing.)* No, don't do that! We need you! Please don't leave me! Please take me home with you.

KAYE NYNE: *(ENTERS LEFT and DOGS revert to normal dog behavior.)* I see you've been getting to know the dogs. What do you think? Have you made a decision?

PETE: *(Conflicted, looks back and forth between the DOGS. They seem to be pleading with him.)* They all do have some very unique qualities.

KAYE NYNE: They certainly do!

PETE: But I'm just not sure about a few things.

KAYE NYNE: If you have any questions, ask away.

PETE: *(Cautious.)* Have you ever noticed any strange or unusual behavior from any of them?

KAYE NYNE: Strange behavior? Like what?

PETE: *(Hesitant.)* Oh, I don't know. Just any behavior that might be unusual for a dog?

KAYE NYNE: *(Thinks.)* Hm. I don't think so. They're just regular dogs as far as I can tell. And I've been around thousands of dogs in my lifetime. Just run-of-the-mill canines. Any one of them would make you a great pet.

PETE: *(Probes a little more.)* Because I was talking to them, you see.

KAYE NYNE: Yes?

PETE: You know, *talking* to them? *(KAYE NYNE looks at him blankly, so PETE gives up.)* Oh, all right. I guess I can't let them stay here and be—well, you know. I may be crazy, but... *(Pauses.)* I guess I'll take them all. *(DOGS perk up. PETE shrugs.)*

KAYE NYNE: *(Surprised.)* All three?

PETE: What the heck! I've got the space. They need a good home. I'll take all three of them. Something tells me they really want to go home with me. *(The DOGS smile and nod.)*

KAYE NYNE: That's excellent! Glad to hear it! I'll finish up the paperwork, and we'll get you on your way. Let's go! *(PETE and the excited DOGS EXIT LEFT. KAYE NYNE lingers behind. Aside.)* Somehow I had a feeling they'd convince you. *(Smiles and winks to the AUDIENCE then EXITS LEFT.)*

· · · · · · ·

5. An Unexpected Visitor

RUNNING TIME: 7 minutes

CAST SIZE: 2M

CAST OF CHARACTERS

DUKE FLYSWATTER .... self-important, dim witted hero wannabe

NO-DUH .... wise old Master of the Forcefield; irritable hermit

SETTING

TIME: The future.

PLACE: The remote jungle camp of No-Duh on the swamp planet of Dogobath.

PROPERTIES

Fire pit, kneepads, rustic cooking pot, large spoon.

An Unexpected Visitor

. . . .

NO-DUH ENTERS LEFT, wearing kneepads and walking on his knees to denote his short stature. He carries a rustic cooking pot and a large spoon. He crosses DOWN CENTER toward a fire pit to prepare his evening meal. He hums contentedly as he putts around. Suddenly, DUKE barrels ON RIGHT, whacking violently at unseen, giant, flying insects. He doesn't notice NO-DUH.

DUKE: *(Stumbles around the campsite as he tries to flee the giant bugs.)* Ahh! Ahhh! These mosquitoes are as big as bats! Take that! And that!

NO-DUH: *(Protects his dinner.)* Hey, hey, hey! What do you think you're doing? Get away from my fire pit! Watch out!

DUKE: *(Notices NO-DUH and jumps back.)* Ahhh! Did you say something? *(Observes NO-DUH closely.)* Ugh! What kind of a strange little creature are you?

NO-DUH: *(Resentful.)* For your information, I am neither "strange" nor a "creature." I may look a little rough around the edges... *(Straightens himself up a bit.)* ... but I wasn't exactly expecting company. And by the way, you're not the best-looking human I've ever seen, either. Now get out of my camp!

DUKE: *(Notices his own appearance.)* I am a little beat-up, I'm afraid. I've been searching through this miserable, disgusting swamp for hours now.

NO-DUH: Hey! This swamp is not disgusting! It's beautiful and serene and, until you so rudely stumbled along, it was a very lovely, peaceful place to reside. Now beat it, human! Go back to where you came from and leave me in peace. *(Goes back to his dinner preparation.)*

DUKE: *(Looks around, helpless.)* For your information, my name is Duke. Duke Flyswatter. And I would go back where I came from, but I have no idea where I left my ship. You see, I have traveled for two light years to reach the planet Dogobath and find the wise, old hermit, No-Duh, who is said to live here. But all I have found so far are giant swamp bugs and an ugly, little creature with a bad temper.

NO-DUH: There you go again, pouring on the charm! I can hear you! I do have feelings, you know! What are you still doing here? Get out!

DUKE: I've come so far. I simply must find the wise, old hermit. He's the Master of the Ancient Secrets and the only being in the universe who can teach me the ways of the Forcefield. Have you seen him? Do you know where he lives?

NO-DUH: Maybe I do. Maybe I don't. If I tell you, will you leave me alone?

DUKE: Show me the way to Master No-Duh, and I will be more than happy to leave you to your filthy existence.

NO-DUH: Okay. It's against my better judgment to tell you. You're a very rude human, but... *(Pauses and sighs deeply.)* I am the wise, old hermit whom you seek.

DUKE: *(Taken aback.)* You? *(Starts to laugh.)* You are the wise, old hermit who holds the Ancient Secrets of the Universe? Little ol' you?! *(Erupts with laughter, so amused he can hardly speak.)* Oh, that's a good one. You're too funny. You! The Master of the Ancient Secrets! The Teacher of the Ways of the Forcefield! That's hysterical.

NO-DUH: *(Crosses his arms and waits.)* Are you quite finished? *(DUKE erupts with laughter again.)* Okay, okay! Never mind. You don't need my help. You clearly know everything, so you might as well go find the great, wise hermit on your own.

DUKE: *(Stops laughing as he reconsiders.)* You mean, you really *are* the great, wise Master? You hold the Secrets of the Forcefield?

NO-DUH: Surprised? I can see by your reaction that I'm not exactly what you expected. My name is No-Duh. I am the wisest being in the all the universe. I know the Secrets of the Ancients, and I am Keeper of the Forcefield. You found me. Aren't you thrilled? Now why are you here, and what do you want?

DUKE: *(Becomes the eager student.)* Oh, great and powerful No-Duh. I have traveled for light years to seek your guidance. I must learn the Ways of the Forcefield to protect my planet and usher in a new age of peace and enlightenment. *(Kneels next to NO-DUH in submission.)* Please, take me on as your apprentice and teach me the ancient wisdom.

NO-DUH: *(Sighs heavily and puts his dinner utensils aside.)* Okay, okay. If I must, I must. Let's get this over with. I've got things to do. Places to go. What do you want to know?

DUKE: *(Thinks.)* Well, first I need to know a little more about laser combat. Just in case I run into some Space Grogs or the evil Giant Mudslop.

NO-DUH: Hm. Okay. Well, show me what you've got. Let me see a few fighting moves.

DUKE: All right. *(Stands up and stretches for a minute.)* Here we go. I can see the evil Giant Mudslop approaching in the distance, so I do one of these. *(Flails and chops at the air around him.)* And I do one of these. *(Strikes the air again and lets out an eerie cry.)* And then I slice him in half with my laser sword!

NO-DUH: Oh, boy. You better hope that Giant Mudslop is half blind and hard of hearing, or you'll be swamp toast! First off, raise your arm a little higher to protect your face from laser flashback. *(DUKE raises his arm higher as he repeats one of his moves.)* Not bad. Now raise your right foot for a little more anti-gravitational balance. *(DUKE repeats the move with his right foot higher. He ends up just looking ridiculous.)* There you go. Not bad for a beginner. You keep working on that, while I go take a nap. *(Turns to leave.)*

DUKE: *(Stops him.)* That is amazing. I'm feeling more confident already. Please, Master, just one more thing before you take your leave for the night. Teach me the Ways of the Forcefield. Teach me to read the minds of others and control the actions of those who threaten me. With this ability, I can save the universe and protect all that is right with the Forcefield.

NO-DUH: Oh, boy. When you put it like that, I guess I have no choice. Stop begging. I'll teach you how it works. It's not that hard, really. Any fool can do it... which is fortunate for you. All right. Bend down here, so I can see what you've got in that head of yours. *(DUKE leans his head down to NO-DUH'S level. NO-DUH reaches out and puts both his hands on DUKE'S head and starts to feel around, reading his thoughts.)* Hmmm. Uh-huh. Uh-huh. Oh, my. No way. Whoa! I didn't expect that! *(Removes his hands and rubs them on his clothes.)* Okay, that's quite enough of your thoughts. Now give me your hand. *(DUKE reaches out a hand, and NO-DUH places it on his own forehead.)* I am going to think of a number, and I want you to tell me what it is. *(Flashes ten fingers in front of DUKE'S face, hoping to speed up the process.)*

DUKE: *(Oblivious.)* Well, let's see. I'm sensing something. Yes, I think I'm picking up on your thoughts. This is amazing! *(Slowly.)* You are thinking of the number... 725!

NO-DUH: Not even close. Try again. And this time, concentrate harder! *(Flashes ten fingers in front of his face again.)*

DUKE: Okay. I can get this. *(Places both hands on NO-DUH'S head.)* I think I'm picking up something. It's a huge number... *(NO-DUH shakes his head.)* Oh. It's not a big number. It's a small number. *(NO-DUH nods and flashes ten fingers frantically.)* It's the number two! *(NO-DUH shakes his head.)* Six? *(NO-DUH shakes his head.)* Five? *(NO-DUH puts up one finger at a time until all ten are revealed.)* Oh, it's ten! You are thinking of the number ten! I got it! I can read minds!

NO-DUH: *(Exhausted.)* I told you it wasn't that hard. Good for you. You're a natural.

DUKE: *(Pulls himself up.)* I feel so empowered! *(Searches for the words.)* So focused! So invincible! I can read minds! With this ability, I will be able to use the Forcefield to protect my planet from all alien invaders. The universe will be safe for generations to come!

NO-DUH: That's wonderful. But if I were you, I'd keep practicing for a while. You just go back to your galaxy, work on your skills, and eventually you will make everything right in the Forcefield. Good luck and good night!

DUKE: Thank you, Master No-Duh. Thank you from the bottom of my heart. I must return to my galaxy and fulfill my destiny. I will never forget you and all I have learned.

NO-DUH: Wonderful. Good luck finding your way out of here. Don't forget to take a left at the black hole and a right at the meteor shower. *(To himself.)* I've got to look for a new uncharted planet. This one's getting too many visitors! *(EXITS LEFT as DUKE, fighting off another giant mosquito, races OFF RIGHT.)*

· · · · · · ·

6. THREE HEADS ARE BETTER THAN ONE

RUNNING TIME: 8 minutes

CAST SIZE: 5E

CAST OF CHARACTERS

RIGHT HEAD ....likes romantic comedies

LEFT HEAD......................prefers science fiction movies

CENTER HEAD.................fan of animated features

TICKET SELLER ....bored teenager who enjoys stopping sneaks

MANAGER.......................movie theater supervisor and devoted company employee

SETTING

The lobby of a local multiplex movie theater.

PROPERTIES

Ticket counter, refreshment counter, popcorn, candy, soda, movie ticket.

OPTIONAL COSTUMING

Large t-shirt with three head holes.

Three Heads Are Better Than One

· · · · · · ·

As the scene begins, the TICKET SELLER is behind a ticket counter CENTER, looking bored. There is a refreshment counter with popcorn, candy, and soda RIGHT. RIGHT HEAD, CENTER HEAD, and LEFT HEAD ENTER LEFT, linked together with arms around each other's waists to form one monster. They walk toward CENTER to the ticket counter, stop, and look up as if reading the marquee.

RIGHT HEAD: Oh, I'm so excited. We haven't been to a movie for such a long time.

LEFT HEAD: I've been dying to see the new *Space Wars* movie—*Space Wars: The Sequel, Part Two*. The CG effects are supposed to be out of this world.

CENTER HEAD: I can't wait to see that new animated feature in 3D—*The Misadventures of the Near-Sighted Cyclops.*

RIGHT HEAD: Ooh! Look at that! Rex Buffman is in that new romantic comedy *One Head, One Heart.* I just love Rex Buffman!

LEFT HEAD: Wait a minute! We're not going to some chick flick!

CENTER HEAD: That's right. We're going to see *The Misadventures of the Near-Sighted Cyclops*! It got two thumbs up.

RIGHT HEAD: What? We're not going to see that animated 3D Cyclops movie!

LEFT HEAD: We certainly are not. We're going to see *Space Wars: the Sequel, Part Two*!

RIGHT HEAD: No, no, no! (*Hugs the center actor as if hugging his/her self.*) I want to see something warm and fuzzy, like a nice romantic comedy! *(All THREE HEADS argue at once.)*

CENTER HEAD: *(Simultaneously.)* I've been waiting all month to see *The Misadventures of the Near-Sighted Cyclops!*

RIGHT HEAD: *(Simultaneously.)* We always go to your shows. It's my turn to choose!

LEFT HEAD: *(Simultaneously.)* I've been waiting all year for the *Space Wars* sequel to come out!

CENTER HEAD: *(Stops the argument.)* Okay, okay! That's enough arguing. We'll just have to settle this like a calm, rational three-headed monster. Okay?

LEFT HEAD/RIGHT HEAD: *(Reluctant.)* Okay. *(Hold out their hands.)*

CENTER HEAD: I'll count to three. Ready? *(As CENTER HEAD counts, RIGHT HEAD and LEFT HEAD pump their fists, preparing to play "Rock, Paper, Scissors.")* One, two, three! *(On "three," LEFT HEAD and RIGHT HEAD both show "scissors." There is no winner, so CENTER HEAD counts again.)* One, two, three! *(LEFT HEAD and RIGHT HEAD both show "rock." CENTER HEAD gets ready to count again.)* Try not to think so much alike this time. One more time. One, two, three! *(LEFT HEAD shows "paper," and RIGHT HEAD shows "rock.")*

LEFT HEAD: *(Celebrates.)* Paper beats rock! I won! I won!

CENTER HEAD: Not so fast, there. *(To RIGHT HEAD.)* Now you play for me. Ready? I'll count again. One, two, three! *(LEFT HEAD shows "scissors" and RIGHT HEAD shows "rock." RIGHT HEAD celebrates this time, mocking LEFT HEAD. Then they realize that CENTER HEAD has won.)* That settles it. We're going to see *The Misadventures of the Near-Sighted Cyclops*. Good work, if I do say so myself. *(LEFT HEAD and RIGHT HEAD sulk as they walk to the ticket booth.)* One ticket for *The Misadventures of the Near-Sighted Cyclops*, please.

TICKET SELLER: One ticket for *The Misadventures of the Near-Sighted Cyclops*. Here you go. *(Hands them a ticket. RIGHT HEAD takes the ticket.)* And what about the rest of you? You want Cyclops tickets, too? *(Looks them up and down.)* I assume you're together.

LEFT HEAD/RIGHT HEAD: *(Still sulking.)* Yeah. We're with him. *(Or her.)*

TICKET SELLER: So, two more tickets to *The Misadventures of the Near-Sighted Cyclops*.

CENTER HEAD: No, we don't need any more tickets. There's only one of us.

TICKET SELLER: Not from where I stand. It looks to me like there are three of you. *(THREE HEADS all laugh.)*

LEFT HEAD: I wish there were three of us! That would make life so much easier.

CENTER HEAD: But there is only one of us.

RIGHT HEAD: That's right, only one of us. *(Sighs heavily. THREE HEADS start to walk RIGHT toward the movie theater.)*

TICKET SELLER: *(Runs out of the booth in front of them.)* Now wait a minute! Wait just a doggone minute! *(Extends both arms out to block their path.)* A lot of people try to sneak into the theater, but no one gets past me without paying for a ticket.

CENTER HEAD: What are you talking about? I did pay! *(RIGHT HEAD waves the ticket in the air.)*

TICKET SELLER: *(Still blocks their path.)* Look, I don't know what kind of underhanded scam you're trying to pull here, but you're not getting away with it on my shift! *(Shouts.)* Manager! I need the manager here! Manager! *(THREE HEADS talk amongst themselves, bewildered.)*

MANAGER: *(ENTERS RIGHT.)* All right, all right. Quiet down, everyone. Is there a problem here? *(TICKET SELLER and THREE HEADS all start explaining at once, ad-libbing their lines. MANAGER waves a hand to stop* *them.)* Please, please. One at a time. One at a time! Let's hear from our valued patrons first, shall we?

THREE HEADS: *(Together.)* Well, you see, I just bought a ticket for *The Near-Sighted Cyclops* movie, and this employee of yours... *(Point to TICKET SELLER.)* ...won't let me go in.

MANAGER: No, no, no. I said one at a time, please.

THREE HEADS: *(Look puzzled. They speak together again.)* We *were* talking one at a time.

MANAGER: No, you weren't. You were all talking at the same time. Now please, one at a time.

THREE HEADS: *(Look at each other, still puzzled. They look around the room to see if there is anyone else besides them talking. RIGHT HEAD and LEFT HEAD shrug their shoulders.)* We *are* talking one at a time!

TICKET SELLER: *(To MANAGER.)* You see? You see? They're trying to make us believe that they are one... *(Hesitates and looks them over.)* ...well, one something or other. I'm not sure what. But it's obvious that they have *three* heads and they should pay for *three* tickets!

MANAGER: *(Finally catches on.)* Oh! I think I see the problem now. *(Walks around the HEADS slowly, assessing the situation.)* My, this is quite a conundrum. May I ask you a couple of questions to clarify the situation?

THREE HEADS: *(Ad-lib)* Okay. I guess that would be all right. Yeah, sure.

MANAGER: How many hearts do you have?

THREE HEADS: *(Consider this, then together.)* One.

MANAGER: Hm. Interesting. And how many stomachs do you have?

RIGHT HEAD: One triple-sized stomach!

MANAGER: I see. And how many legs do you have? *(THREE HEADS all start counting their legs.)*

CENTER HEAD: Six!

MANAGER: Oh, my. And how many brains do you have?

THREE HEADS: *(Unenthusiastic.)* Three.

MANAGER: I see. Well, this is a dilemma, isn't it? One heart, one stomach, six legs, and three brains.

TICKET SELLER: Exactly! Three brains! That's why they should pay for three tickets. *(THREE HEADS shake their heads simultaneously.)*

MANAGER: On the other hand, they have only one heart, so perhaps they should buy only one ticket. *(THREE HEADS nod simultaneously.)* Will you all share the same seat?

THREE HEADS: Of course.

MANAGER: *(Paces.)* You'll sit in one seat, but you'll watch the movie with three sets of eyes. This is most confusing. There is nothing about how to handle a situation like this in the *Theater Manager's Handbook*, so I'll just have to make the decision myself. But I don't want to act in haste and make the wrong decision. *(Still paces.)* I mean, three heads really *should* pay for three tickets, shouldn't they? Regardless of how many hearts and stomachs they have. That makes the most sense, doesn't it? Hmmm. *(THREE HEADS exchange concerned looks.)*

CENTER HEAD: Look, maybe we can help simplify this for you.

RIGHT HEAD: Yes, it's actually much easier than you are making it out to be.

LEFT HEAD: It's true that, as a three-headed monster, we have only one heart.

CENTER HEAD: And only one stomach.

RIGHT HEAD: Six legs and three brains.

LEFT HEAD: But when we put our heads together, there is one more thing we share.

CENTER HEAD: *(Louder.)* One really monstrous temper!

THREE HEADS: *(Rise up, becoming as big and intimidating as possible. In booming and angry voices.)* Now let me into the movie theater! *(MANAGER and TICKET SELLER hang onto each other and start to shake, cowering out of the way. THREE HEADS are quite pleased with themselves. LEFT HEAD gives RIGHT HEAD a high-five as they strut past MANAGER and TICKET SELLER, then they stop and turn back.)*

CENTER HEAD: Oh, and I'll take one humongous-sized popcorn, please. *(Confers with the OTHER HEADS.)* Butter?

LEFT HEAD: That would be lovely.

RIGHT HEAD: And maybe a large box of Skittles.

CENTER HEAD: Oh, yes! Skittles sound good. And a soda, too. An extra large soda with three straws, please! You can bring the refreshments to me in the theater.

LEFT HEAD: I don't want to miss the coming attractions!

RIGHT HEAD: I'll be sitting in the front row! *(THREE HEADS EXIT RIGHT. TICKET SELLER and MANAGER scramble behind the concessions counter to fulfill the order.)*

· · · · · · ·

7. The Nuts and Bolts of Charm School

RUNNING TIME: 10 minutes

CAST SIZE: 1F, 3E

CAST OF CHARACTERS

C-25............................enrolled in the class to learn
                manners
D-94............................sent for etiquette training
R3-D3..........................needs social refinement
MS. DEANGELO..............teacher at The Nuts and Bolts
                Charm School

SETTING

A classroom.

PROPERTIES

Three chairs, sign that reads: "The Nuts and Bolts Charm School," clipboard.

The Nuts and Bolts of Charm School

· · · · · · ·

There are three chairs LEFT and a sign CENTER with the school's name. D-94 and R3-D3 are seated in chairs LEFT. C-25 ENTERS RIGHT and looks around. All the robots move stiffly and speak primarily in a monotone voice with mechanically clipped diction. C-25 crosses LEFT to the OTHER ROBOTS, who stand to meet him.

C-25: I assume this is The Nuts and Bolts Charm School? You must be my fellow classmates. I am Vexar 500 Customizable Robot Companion, model number C-25, but you can just call me C-25.

D-94: *(Matter-of-fact.)* I am Universally Mobile, Semi-Humanoid Robot, model number D-94. I come equipped with cameras, sensors, audio, and a digital touchscreen interface. You can refer to me as D-94.

R3-D3: I am Intergalactic Customizable Protocol Drone, model number R3-D3. I am designed to integrate efficiency, etiquette, and smart home management. You may alert my sensors by referring to me as R3-D3. *(ROBOTS shuffle around, reading data about each other by touching a hand to each other's foreheads.)*

MS. DEANGELO: *(ENTERS RIGHT, carrying a clipboard. Cheerful and only slightly robotic.)* I see you're getting to know each other. Very good. Can you please take your seats? *(ROBOTS shuffle back to the chairs, moving from seat to seat.)* That's right. Just take a seat—any seat will do. Just sit. All right, there is good. Just sit down. That's fine. Just sit. Sit! *(ROBOTS finally settle down and come to attention.)* There. That's fine. Thank you, and welcome to The Nuts and Bolts Charm School. My name is Ms. DeAngelo, and I will be your instructor today. I'd like to start by taking attendance. *(Refers to her clipboard.)* Let's see now, is C-25 present?

C-25: *(Raises a hand.)* I am present and at your service.

MS. DEANGELO: Thank you, C-25. And is R3-D3 here?

R3-D3: *(Raises a hand.)* Affirmative. Present and accounted for.

MS. DEANGELO: Thank you, R3-D3. And last but not least, D-94?

D-94: Correct. You have called me last, but I am certainly not the least. I am a Universally Mobile, Semi-Humanoid Robot, model number D-94. I come equipped with cameras, sensors, audio, and a digital touchscreen interface. You can simply refer to me as D-94.

MS. DEANGELO: Thank you, D-94. I will do that.

D-94: Do what?

MS. DEANGELO: I will call you D-94.

D-94: *(Repeats.)* You can call me D-94. I am a Universally Mobile, Semi-Humanoid Robot, model number D-94. I come equipped with cameras, sensors, audio, and a digital touchscreen interface. But you can simply refer to me as D-94.

MS. DEANGELO: Thank you, D-94. I understand, and I appreciate your thoroughness. Let's move on! Your owners have enrolled you all in The Nuts and Bolts Charm School. *(ROBOTS look at each other, confused.)* You are all advanced robotic systems with multiple skill sets and advanced data potential, but your owners have determined that you need some additional programming to fulfill your current positions. So we are here today to learn and program you for success. Are you all on board? *(ROBOTS still look puzzled, but MS. DEANGELO doesn't seem to notice.)* You all work in very important households. You are companions and servants to dignitaries, celebrities, ambassadors, and politicians. Impeccable etiquette and flawless manners are of the utmost importance in your lines of work, and apparently, there are several areas in which you need to improve. So let's start by learning a simple, polite bow, shall we? Would you stand, please? *(ROBOTS stand in a straight line.)* When you are introduced to a human, it is considered polite to say "hello" or "how do you do?" and perform a little bowing gesture as a sign of respect. This is how we bow politely. *(Demonstrates a nice, deep, slow bow. ROBOTS seem impressed.)* Now you try, R3-D3. Would you bow for us, please?

R3-D3: *(Steps forward.)* How do you do? *(Bows slowly and deeply, flopping all the way forward toward the ground.)*

MS. DEANGELO: *(Helps him stand upright again.)* That may be bowing a little too far. Try about half that far over.

R3-D3: How do you do? *(Bows again, halfway this time.)*

MS. DEANGELO: *(Claps.)* Very nice, R3-D3. That's just fine. *(R3-D3 steps back into line.)* What about you, D-94?

D-94: *(Steps forward.)* Hello. How do you do? *(Flails arms around uncontrollably while bowing forward several times.)* Hello. How do you do? Hello. How do you do? *(The OTHER ROBOTS take cover behind their chairs.)*

MS. DEANGELO: *(Grabs at D-94'S flailing arms.)* Okay, D-94. That's enough. Stop! Stop! You don't swing your arms when you bow. Your arms just stay at your sides, like this. *(Places D-94'S hands at his sides, and he stops flailing as she demonstrates. D-94 tries again, forcing his hands to stay at his sides. He manages a fairly respectable bow and seems pleased.)* There. That's better. You see? *(D-94 steps back into line.)* Maybe we should come back to the bowing later. Let's move on to social human pleasantries. Why don't we try practicing some polite small talk, shall we?

C-25: Please clarify, Instructor. What is "small talk"? How can talk be minuscule? Is this similar to microscopic interfacing?

MS. DEANGELO: That is a very good question, C-25. "Small talk" is the polite conversation humans engage in as they are getting to know each other. It may include comments about the weather or compliments about one's appearance. Nothing too heavy or serious. Shall we try? Why don't I have a conversation with C-25, and we will start with some small talk. Imagine I am an important dignitary at one of your embassy dinners. Okay, you may begin.

C-25: *(Steps forward and does a nice bow.)* Hello. How do you do, Ambassador? You are looking very bald tonight.

MS. DEANGELO: *(Stops him.)* No, no! I'm sorry, C-25. You shouldn't say anything about the ambassador's bald head.

C-25: But I was making a comment on his appearance. It is a nice, shiny, bald head. Very distinguished, I believe.

MS. DEANGELO: I'm sure you meant no harm, but it is possible that the ambassador is sensitive about his bald head and does not want it noticed.

C-25: I do not understand. It is shiny and smooth, like an enormous ball bearing. It is impossible not to notice it.

MS. DEANGELO: Just the same, let's not talk about the ambassador's bald head. Try talking about something less personal.

C-25: *(Computes for a moment then tries again.)* Hello. How do you do, Mrs. Ambassador? My, you are looking very sour and dim-witted tonight.

MS. DEANGELO: Oh, boy. I don't think that's going to work, either.

C-25: I was just making an honest observation about the ambassador's wife.

MS. DEANGELO: Well, in this case, honesty may not be the best policy. Let's move on and try something else, shall we? Sometimes in social situations it may be necessary to lighten the mood or create a humorous moment to entertain the guests. Why don't we try telling a little joke or two?

R3-D3: *(Raises a hand, enthusiastic.)* Oh, I know a joke! I know a joke! May I create a humorous social moment by telling my unusually witty quip?

MS. DEANGELO: Certainly R3-D3. Tell us your witty joke.

R3-D3: A cyborg and an android walk into a coffee shop. *(C-25 and D-94 interrupt with robotic laughter.)*

D-94: Oh! I love this one!

C-25: Hysterical! You tell it so well!

R3-D3: *(Continues.)* The waiter says, "We don't serve robots!" And the android says, "Oh…"

ALL ROBOTS: *(Together.)* "But someday you will!" *(Laugh hysterically.)*

MS. DEANGELO: *(Tries to quiet them down.)* All right. Yes, yes, very funny. Very funny. But I don't think it's a good idea—

C-25: *(Interrupts.)* What about this wacky antic? A human is eating a bowl of soup at a fancy restaurant. Suddenly, he calls out, "Waiter, waiter! What's this robot doing in my soup?" And the waiter says, "It looks like he's performing tasks twice as well as humans because he knows no fear or pain." *(ROBOTS erupt in loud laughter again.)*

MS. DEANGELO: *(Works to quiet them down. C-25 and R3-D3 continue to giggle softly, but D-94 cannot stop laughing. He seems to be stuck in a high-speed, repetitive mode.)* D-94! D-94! Please, stop laughing!

R3-D3: His receptors are not responding to your voice commands.

C-25: We must restart his operating system to restore normal circuit functions.

MS. DEANGELO: Are you sure? What if something goes wrong?

R3-D3: If we do not restart his operating system, he may sustain permanent corruption to his motherboard.

C-25: Yes, his entire data system will be lost, causing irreparable damage. You must push his restart button now. Before it is too late to save him.

MS. DEANGELO: *(Very nervous and hesitant.)* Oh, all right. Here goes nothing! *(Pushes D-94'S restart button. D-94 collapses forward at the waist and becomes still.)* Oh, no. I broke him!

D-94: *(Begins to twitch and gyrate, eventually coming to a standing position. He appears calm and in control once again.)* Greetings. I am a Universally Mobile, Semi-Humanoid Robot, model number D-94. I come equipped with cameras, sensors, audio, and a digital touchscreen interface. You can simply refer to me as D-94. How do you do? *(Bows politely.)*

C-25: Mission accomplished.

MS. DEANGELO: *(Heaves a sigh of relief. ROBOTS return to their seats as she composes herself.)* Thank you, everybody, for helping with that challenging situation. I think we may have had enough etiquette for one day. I hope you have learned a little something in my class. Using good manners and fine social skills can set you above the average robot. Exciting doors of opportunity will open to you as your new skills continue to blossom. There is just one more thing I want to share with you today. Something that I believe you have not determined for yourselves. I, too, am a robot—a Vexar Android, model number 626-B9, to be precise. I bet you couldn't even tell. *(ROBOTS sit up straight and look surprised.)* It's true. I was once like you, and through diligent practice, I have been able to become convincingly humanoid. I believe it is very difficult for most people and most robots to determine whether I am actually robotic or simply a human. *(ROBOTS are* *quite enthralled. They stand and move slowly toward MS. DEANGELO, studying her intently. They all begin trying to impress her.)*

C-25: Hello. How do you do? You are looking very well-polished tonight. Did you recently get your head-piece replaced? It looks like new. Would you like to go to the Jiffy-Lube with me sometime?

R3-D3: Hello. Your hair looks so shiny and metallic. Would you like to see me bow? *(Bows repeatedly.)* Perhaps we can micro-interface at your place later? Where is your charging station?

D-94: How are you this evening? I would like to tell you a joke, please. Two robots walked into a laundromat. *(Laughs.)* Very funny, don't you agree? A laundromat? Ha, ha, ha! I have a million of them. Do you like a droid with a good sense of humor?

MS. DEANGELO: No, please. I didn't mean... Could you all just sit down? Please go back to your seats. All right, that's it! Back off, or I'll push all your sleep buttons! *(Realizes her threats aren't working.)* Class dismissed! *(Runs OFF RIGHT as ROBOTS chase after her.)*

· · · · · · ·

8. Ready, Set, Duel

RUNNING TIME: 6 minutes

CAST SIZE: 4M, 1E

CAST OF CHARACTERS

FUMBELDOR .... a wizard of extraordinary skill
LARRY .... eager apprentice of Fumbeldor
SANDGOLF .... another wizard with remarkable talent
ROLO .... fumbling apprentice of Sandgolf
REFEREE .... official for the Wizard's Duel

SETTING

A clearing in the woods.

PROPERTIES

Two pillows, three sticks, scroll, whistle, coin.

Ready, Set, Duel

· · · · · · ·

FUMBELDOR: *(ENTERS LEFT with LARRY, who is carrying a pillow with a stick on top like a ring bearer. Looks around.)* Are you sure this is the spot?

LARRY: Yes, oh great Fumbeldor, sir.

FUMBELDOR: And this is the correct time for the meeting?

LARRY: Yes, oh great Fumbeldor, sir.

FUMBELDOR: *(Smug.)* It looks like Sandgolf the Great was too frightened to show up for the Wizard's Duel, as I expected.

SANDGOLF: *(ENTERS RIGHT with ROLO, who is also carrying a pillow with a stick on it.)* Surely you jest! Me? Frightened by your rusty, old wizard skills? Don't make me laugh. *(Laughs a hearty laugh.)*

ROLO: Don't make him laugh! *(Laughs until SANDGOLF gives him a stern look)* Sorry, sir. Just trying to help.

FUMBELDOR: So you had the guts to show up after all. I am surprised.

SANDGOLF: Fumbeldor, my old nemesis. How brave of you to show up. Or should I say, how crazy of you to show up? For surely you will meet a grisly fate this fine morning.

FUMBELDOR: *(Laughs.)* Oh, Sandgolf. Your bravado does amuse me. I am afraid it is you who will meet your fate today. It is so sad that you shall not live to tell about it. But don't worry, I shall tell the world! *(They circle each other like two animals about to strike.)*

REFEREE: *(ENTERS RIGHT, carrying a scroll and a stick. He has a coin in his pocket and blows a whistle.)* All right, all right. That's enough of that. Back off, you two. *(WIZARDS back away with FUMBELDOR UP LEFT and SANDGOLF UP RIGHT, standing by their APPRENTICES, who are still holding the pillows and sticks.)* That's better. Let's get on with this. I have to referee a Quidditch match in thirty minutes, and I don't want to be late. *(Reads from the scroll as the WIZARDS do various warm-ups and stretches.)* "My dear, honorable wizards, welcome. You have challenged each other to this very serious duel, and ye shall abide by the governing rules that were set forth by the Imminent Council of Wizards in the year 1052." Do all who are involved agree to the terms? If so, say "Aye."

SANDGOLF/ROLO/FUMBELDOR/LARRY: *(Together.)* Aye.

REFEREE: Do any here disagree? *(No response.)* Then on behalf of The Imminent Council, your request for a duel is accepted. Please listen carefully as I read the official rules. Rule number one—No disappearing. Rule number two—No irreversible spells. Rule number three—No unreasonable taunting or excessive celebration. Rule number four—Only one animal from any species may be conjured during any one duel. And finally, rule number five—No unsportsmanlike conduct. Do you who are about to duel agree to the rules as stated? If so, say "Aye."

SANDGOLF/FUMBELDOR: *(A little disappointed, together.)* Aye.

REFEREE: *(Puts the scroll in a pocket.)* Excellent. The rules have been accepted by both parties, and the duel can begin. Each wizard shall stay on his side of the clearing. I see that you have each brought an apprentice. The apprentices shall step forward at this time. *(The WIZARDS take the sticks as wands, and the APPRENTICES put down the pillows. The APPRENTICES step forward and shake hands with each other as the WIZARDS swing their sticks around, preparing to conjure.)* Each wizard in turn shall transform his apprentice into the creature of his choice. Only one transformation per turn. When I feel there is a clear winner, I shall call the duel. The referee's decision is final. Wizards, step forward for the coin toss. *(WIZARDS step forward.)* Sandgolf, please make your call when the coin is in the air. *(Takes a coin from a pocket and flips it into the air.)*

SANDGOLF: Heads!

REFEREE: *(Catches the coin and flips it onto the back of a hand, then looks.)* It is heads. *(To SANDGOLF.)* How do you wish to proceed?

SANDGOLF: I shall conjure first.

REFEREE: *(Announces.)* Sandgolf the Great has chosen to conjure first. *(Steps back with FUMBELDOR. APPRENTICES remain at CENTER.)*

SANDGOLF: *(Becomes very focused and intense, then weaves his spell on ROLO.)* Abracadabra, fumble and bumble. You shall become the king of the jungle! *(ROLO roars and acts like a lion, circling the stage and eyeing LARRY, ready to pounce.)*

FUMBELDOR: *(Steps forward and places a spell on LARRY.)* Arsenic-canoodle, fiddle-ee-fee. You shall become a near-sighted bee. *(LARRY buzzes around the stage as a bee and flies at ROLO, tormenting him. ROLO bats at LARRY furiously.)*

SANDGOLF: *(Steps forward and places a new spell on ROLO.)* Higgledy-piggledy, beaver and skunk. You are a giant with ears and a trunk! *(ROLO morphs into a huge elephant, using one arm as his trunk. He whacks at LARRY and sends him hurling across the stage, then stomps around.)*

FUMBELDOR: *(Prepares his next spell for LARRY.)* Rickety-snickety, leech, fly, and louse. Now you shall triumph as a tiny, gray mouse. *(LARRY morphs into a squeaking mouse. He runs in and around ROLO'S legs, nearly toppling him. Terrified, ROLO tries to flee.)*

SANDGOLF: *(Prepares his next spell.)* Storm clouds on high, tornados that howl. Lick your long whiskers, and pounce with "meow!" *(ROLO morphs into a spitting cat and chases LARRY around the stage.)*

FUMBELDOR: *(Raises a hand.)* Objection! That's not fair. *(The REFEREE whistles and calls a time-out.)* He already conjured a lion. He can't produce a cat. They are both members of the feline family!

SANDGOLF: *(Taunts.)* What's the matter? Can't handle the heat of the competition? What? Are you scared? Afraid your cute, little mousey might get devoured? *(Does a victory dance, resembling a touchdown dance.)*

FUMBELDOR: *(Points at SANDGOLF.)* Taunting! Taunting! Unsportsmanlike conduct! Excessive celebration, and he hasn't even won!

SANDGOLF: *(Flaps around like a chicken, clucks, and chants.)* Chicken! Chicken! Fumbeldor's a chicken!

REFEREE: *(Blows the whistle, but the WIZARDS keep arguing. Casts a spell.)* Taunt and argue, dreadful moan. Turn these wizards to pillars of stone. *(WIZARDS suddenly FREEZE. LARRY and ROLO return to normal and fall to the floor. REFEREE walks to the WIZARDS and taps on them, then helps the APPRENTICES get up.)* Are you guys okay? That was quite a duel, wasn't it? Hey, how would you two like to go to a Quidditch match while these wizards cool off? I can get you in for free. *(APPRENTICES ad-lib excitement about this idea.)* Excellent! Let's get out of here. *(REFEREE, LARRY, and ROLO EXIT RIGHT, leaving SANDGOLF and FUMBLEDOR FROZEN ONSTAGE.)*

• • • • • • •

9. Happy Birthday, Captain Dirk

RUNNING TIME: 8 minutes

CAST SIZE: 2M, 3E

CAST OF CHARACTERS

CAPTAIN DIRK .... dashing captain with a sweet
           tooth
LIEUTENANT YOU-WHO ..... sentimental communications
           officer
MR. SCHLOCK .... highly logical first officer
LIEUTENANT LU-LU .... no-nonsense helmsman
DOCTOR KILJOY .... chief medical officer;
           cholesterol cop

SETTING

TIME: The future.

PLACE: The bridge of the USS Intergalactic Spaceship,
deep in outer space.

PROPERTIES

Five chairs, two long tables or counters, keyboard,
microphone.

Happy Birthday, Captain Dirk

· · · · · · ·

At the opening of the scene, the empty captain's chair sits CENTER with two chairs to either side behind long tables or counters, all facing the AUDIENCE, where there is an imaginary screen. The CREW MEMBERS are ONSTAGE, hard at work at their different stations. LU-LU sits LEFT from the captain's chair, seated next to YOU-WHO, who types away on a keyboard. SCHLOCK sits RIGHT from the captain's chair with a microphone, seated next to KILJOY.

CAPTAIN: *(ENTERS LEFT and speaks with great authority.)* Good morning, crew.

CREW: *(Together.)* Good morning, Captain.

CAPTAIN: *(Sits in the captain's chair.)* Lieutenant You-Who, I am ready to dictate.

YOU-WHO: Yes, Captain. *(Types into the keyboard as the CAPTAIN speaks.)*

CAPTAIN: Entry into Captain's Diary, intergalactic date one-seven-one-four-point-one. Our current position— Orbiting Planet Q-one-four-one. Onboard the USS Intergalactic Spaceship—Captain Dirk, in command. Mr. Schlock, first officer. Doctor Kiljoy, chief medical officer. Lieutenant Lu-Lu, chief helmsman, and Lieutenant You-Who, chief communications officer. Our mission—To investigate an unidentifiable object orbiting Planet Q-one-four-one. End dictation. Did you get that, You-Who?

YOU-WHO: Yes, Captain. Diary entry recorded.

SCHLOCK: *(Approaches CAPTAIN.)* Captain, I could not help noticing that this particular intergalactic date— one-seven-one-four-point-one—coincides with the day of your birth. Happy birthday, Captain.

CREW: Happy birthday, Captain.

SCHLOCK: Pardon me for not appearing more jovial, Captain, but I have spent a lifetime learning to suppress my emotions. This is as happy as I get.

CAPTAIN: I know that, Schlock, and thank you, everyone. It is very kind of you to remember. Perhaps we can celebrate later in the officer's quarters.

ALL CREW: *(Ad-lib responses.)* Yes, sir. Excellent, sir. That would be wonderful, sir.

CAPTAIN: *(Gets back to the task at hand.)* Lieutenant Lu-Lu, what do we know about the unidentifiable object that is orbiting Planet Q-one-four-one?

LU-LU: The object is orbiting at a varying rate and speed, Captain. This would indicate that it is not cylindrical but has an odd, uneven shape.

CAPTAIN: We had better get a closer look, Lu-Lu. Warp factor six. Full speed ahead.

LU-LU: Yes, sir. Warp factor six. All engines powered on.

CAPTAIN: What is your opinion on this mysterious object, Mr. Schlock?

SCHLOCK: My opinion, sir, is that we must approach with great caution. We have no idea what matter it contains or where it has come from. According to my calculations, there is a one in two thousand chance it might be out to destroy the USS Intergalactic Spaceship.

CAPTAIN: Thank you, Mr. Schlock. Your advice is noted.

KILJOY: Captain, as chief medical officer, I want to remind you that you have your yearly physical today.

CAPTAIN: I don't need a physical, Kiljoy. I am in perfect health. Fit as a fiddle.

KILJOY: A bass fiddle, perhaps, sir. You have put on a little weight this year, and you need to have a check-up. You've developed quite a sweet tooth lately.

CAPTAIN: Don't be ridiculous, Kiljoy. So I've put on a few pounds. I'm still the picture of health. Wouldn't you agree, Schlock?

SCHLOCK: If by, "the picture of health" you mean "an overweight man with high cholesterol and hypertension," then I agree completely, sir. You are the picture of health.

KILJOY: Bad health, that is.

LU-LU: *(Excited.)* Captain! We have visual contact with the object, sir!

CAPTAIN: Bring it up on the screen, Lu-Lu. *(CAPTAIN and CREW stare forward.)*

YOU-WHO: What is it, Captain?

CAPTAIN: It's impossible to tell at this distance, Lu-Lu. Full speed ahead.

SCHLOCK: I recommend caution, Captain.

LU-LU: Range two hundred light years and closing.

CAPTAIN: Lock phasers on the object, Lu-Lu.

LU-LU: Phasers locked, sir.

YOU-WHO: Captain, I am picking up a strange humming sound from the object.

CAPTAIN: Can you identify it, You-Who?

YOU-WHO: I can't make it out. The object is still too far in the distance.

CAPTAIN: *(Excited.)* Lu-Lu, what is our current range?

LU-LU: One hundred and eighty light years and closing, sir.

KILJOY: Captain Dirk, I must warn you about your blood pressure, sir. Please, stay calm.

CAPTAIN: How can I stay calm at a time like this, Kiljoy? Full speed ahead, Lu-Lu!

LU-LU: Yes, sir. Warp factor eight. All power maximum. Hold on to your seats, everyone! *(Cranks up the speed.*

The CAPTAIN and CREW shake and shudder. When they stop shaking, they are near their goal.)

KILJOY: *(Points to the imaginary screen.)* There it is, Captain.

SCHLOCK: What a strange, irregular object. It's spinning and wobbling at a frantic rate.

CAPTAIN: Lock phasers on target, Lu-Lu.

LU-LU: Phasers locked and ready, sir. One thousand meters and closing.

YOU-WHO: The humming noise is stronger now, sir. *(Begins to softly imitate the humming to the tune of "Happy Birthday," but the others don't notice.)*

KILJOY: The object is slowing down its rotation, Captain. I'm beginning to see the shape more clearly.

SCHLOCK: Caution is advised, Captain. The object may be dangerous.

CAPTAIN: *(Watches the object intensely, almost as if he is hypnotized.)* What is this strange object? I feel abnormally attracted to it. *(Starts to reach his hand out toward the screen.)* I want to hold it and—

LU-LU: Captain, the object seems to have some sort of magnetic hold over the ship. We are being pulled toward it. I can't hold the ship!

SCHLOCK: *(Into the microphone.)* Security alert! Security alert! All personnel, code red!

CAPTAIN: *(Still in a trance.)* Come here, little object. Come to Daddy...

YOU-WHO: Captain! I think I have figured out the humming sound. It's... It's... the "Happy Birthday" song.

KILJOY: *(Studies the object on the screen.)* Well, I'll be! The object is a giant cupcake with whipped cream frosting and chocolate sprinkles on top!

CAPTAIN: *(Still in a trance, talks in a sing-song manner.)* Come here, little cupcake. I'm not going to hurt you.

SCHLOCK: *(Urgent.)* Captain, if the whipped cream frosting gets in our engines, we'll be destroyed! Those chocolate sprinkles could cause a chain reaction and disintegrate the entire ship!

KILJOY: Captain Dirk! Captain Dirk! Snap out of it, Captain! You've got to do something!

CAPTAIN: *(Comes to his senses.)* You're right, Kiljoy! I've got to do something before it's too late!

LU-LU: Shall I obliterate the giant cupcake with the phasers, sir?

CAPTAIN: No, Lu-Lu. I have a better idea. I am going to transport myself over to that delicious cupcake and eat it into oblivion! I will sacrifice my health and well-being for the sake of the ship and crew! The captain is going down with the cupcake! *(Runs OFF RIGHT.)*

KILJOY: *(Follows him OFF RIGHT.)* No, Captain, no! Remember your cholesterol!

SCHLOCK: *(Points to the screen, as if he sees the CAPTAIN.)* There he is! The captain has successfully transported himself to the giant cupcake. Amazing. He's going at it with incredible efficiency. There go the sprinkles! *(CREW watches the screen and is repulsed.)*

CREW: *(Ad-lib.)* Ugh! Yuck! That's disgusting! Gross.

SCHLOCK: Well, he did it. He finished off the cupcake so that not a crumb can hurt the ship.

YOU-WHO: *(Sniffles.)* That was the most heroic thing I have ever seen.

LU-LU: That was the most disgusting thing I have ever seen. *(CAPTAIN staggers ON RIGHT with KILJOY.)*

KILJOY: *(Helps the CAPTAIN cross to his chair at CENTER.)* We beamed him back just in time!

YOU-WHO: Captain! You did it! You did it!

CAPTAIN: *(Feels rather sick.)* Yes, You-Who. I did it. And now I would appreciate it if no one ever mentioned cupcakes again.

CREW: Yes, sir.

CAPTAIN: Or chocolate sprinkles.

CREW: Yes, sir.

CAPTAIN: Or my birthday.

CREW: Yes, sir.

CAPTAIN: *(Still sick.)* You-Who, add to Captain's Diary, intergalactic date one-seven-one-four-point-one. The unidentifiable object orbiting Planet Q-one-four-one was found to be an innocent ball of space dust. It has been dematerialized. Over and out.

YOU-WHO: Recorded, Captain.

CAPTAIN: *(Gets up slowly.)* Now, crew, I am going to take a nice birthday nap.

KILJOY: *(Helps CAPTAIN by the arm.)* Right after you have your nice birthday physical, Captain. *(CAPTAIN moans in pain as they EXIT LEFT. CREW gets back to work.)*

· · · · · · ·

10. The Amoeba

RUNNING TIME: 6 minutes

CAST SIZE: 1M, 1F, 4E, unlimited extras

CAST OF CHARACTERS

NARRATOR.....................typical 1950s horror movie
trailer announcer
BOBBY..........................adventurous teenage boy
SUZIE...........................innocent, smart teenage girl
OFFICER SMITH...............local police chief in Sunnydale,
USA
OFFICER JONES...............Smith's right-hand officer
DR. HERMAN ....curious biologist
THE AMOEBA ....unidentifiable, growing monster
from outer space

SETTING

TIME: 1950s.

PLACE: A lonely country road, police station, and Dr. Herman's office.

PROPERTIES

Cup of water.

SOUND EFFECTS

Explosion.

The Amoeba

. . . .

A bare stage is used for each location. The first location is a lonely country road. NARRATOR is DOWN RIGHT throughout the scene, stepping back when not speaking. BOBBY and SUZIE ENTER LEFT on an evening stroll.

NARRATOR: *(Steps forward.)* It was just a peaceful Sunday evening in the quiet little town of Sunnydale, USA, when suddenly, a huge flash of light barreled across the sky.

BOBBY: *(Looks up and points toward AUDIENCE.)* What's that?

SUZIE: It looks like a shooting star. *(SOUND EFFECT: EXPLOSION.)*

BOBBY: Boy, Suzie. That was awfully close. I think it landed in old Farmer Johnson's wheat field. Come on. Let's go see if we can find out what it was. *(Starts to EXIT RIGHT.)*

SUZIE: *(Grabs his arm.)* Wait, Bobby! Are you sure we should? Maybe we should just go tell someone.

BOBBY: But Suzie, if we leave, we might not find it again. C'mon, let's go! It landed over there in that field. *(Runs OFF RIGHT with SUZIE.)*

NARRATOR: *(Steps forward.)* What is this mysterious ball of fire that landed in Farmer Johnson's field? What will Bobby and Suzie find when they get there? Take care, good people of Earth. Your world may never be the same again! *(Scene continues in the town's police station. OFFICERS SMITH and JONES ENTER LEFT.)*

BOBBY: *(Runs ON RIGHT, followed by SUZIE. Urgent.)* Officer Smith! Officer Smith! You have to come right away!

OFFICER SMITH: Hey there, young man. Slow down a minute. What's the emergency?

BOBBY: It's old Farmer Johnson!

SUZIE: He's been eaten alive by a gross and disgusting monster!

OFFICER JONES: Now wait just a minute, you two. Is this some sort of teenage prank?

BOBBY: No, sir! We saw it with our own four eyes. It was terrible.

OFFICER SMITH: Well, what was it? What did it look like?

SUZIE: It was slimy and creepy...

BOBBY: ...and it didn't have any arms or legs, but it sucked old Farmer Johnson in with these jelly-like feelers and ate him whole! Then it started to grow. It grew bigger and bigger!

OFFICER SMITH: *(Suspicious.)* And just what were you two kids doing over at old Farmer Johnson's place, anyway?

SUZIE: *(Innocent.)* We were just out for a walk. We were watching the stars, and we saw a flash of light like a meteor shooting down from the sky. It landed in old Farmer Johnson's field, so we went to investigate.

BOBBY: Suzie's right. We just wanted to see the meteor, but we saw a hideous monster instead!

SUZIE: It looked like a giant amoeba with a big, black nucleus and slimy ectoplasm.

BOBBY: You've got to believe her, Officer. Suzie is a straight-"A" student. She knows what she's talking about. Come on, we've got to get back to the farm before the monster heads for town. *(He, SUZIE and OFFICERS run OFF RIGHT.)*

NARRATOR: *(Steps forward.)* What is this unearthly monster that has descended upon our peaceful planet? Where has it come from? What does it want? Is Suzie really a straight-"A" student? The officers will soon discover that not even their most sophisticated arsenal of weapons can destroy or contain this creature. How can it be stopped? People of Earth, beware! *(The scene is now the office of DR. HERMAN, who ENTERS LEFT with a small cup of water. OFFICER SMITH, BOBBY, and SUZIE ENTER RIGHT.)*

OFFICER SMITH: *(Frantic.)* It was awful, Dr. Herman. That creature is alive! I beat at it with a stick and tried to shoot it with my revolver, but it just kept coming at me in this giant, slimy, morphing shape. It was horrifying! It had one strange, black eye in the middle of its body. It looked and moved like Jell-O, with hairy feelers that stretched out to grab me. It was hideous, I tell you! Hideous!

DR. HERMAN: *(Splashes the water on OFFICER SMITH'S face.)* Get a hold of yourself, Officer Smith! You're becoming hysterical!

NARRATOR: *(Steps forward.)* What is this horrifying creature that has come to consume the people of Earth? If the citizens of the small town of Sunnydale, USA discover the truth, mass hysteria will break out and spread throughout the country, and then around the world. Can the monster be stopped before it's too late? *(OFFICER JONES staggers ON RIGHT and collapses. The OTHERS run over.)*

DR. HERMAN: *(Kneels next to OFFICER JONES.)* What is it, Officer Jones? What happened? What did you see?

OFFICER JONES: *(Exhausted.)* It was pitch black. I couldn't see anything. Then I heard a horrifying scream and headed toward it. Suddenly, something slimy and cold reached out and touched my arm. It tried to suck me in through its skin, but I managed to get away. It was the most frightening thing I've ever experienced.

DR. HERMAN: *(Stands and considers this.)* Do you realize what this is? You have described a giant, man-eating amoeba. A single-celled being from another planet that has come to consume the people of Earth. And if this *is* a giant, man-eating amoeba, it will divide and multiply, growing bigger and bigger, and we will be unable to stop it. Our only hope is to somehow communicate with the creature. Then we may not only save the earth, but unlock the mysteries of the universe, as well.

OFFICER SMITH: But if we can't communicate with it, we will be its next meal!

DR. HERMAN: An amoeba has a very primitive brain called a nucleus. We must try to communicate with this monster's nucleus before it's too late. Maybe we can use the universal language of hand signals. Come on! *(ALL run OFF RIGHT with OFFICER SMITH supporting OFFICER JONES.)*

NARRATOR: *(Steps forward.)* These are only the first people to see the hideous one-celled monster. Will the creature's insatiable appetite soon swallow the entire population of the world? Or will the amoeba eat everyone in Sunnydale, USA, decide it's full, and go back to its own planet? Is this the end of the earth as we know it? Don't miss *The Amoeba. (Cheery all of a sudden.)* Coming this holiday season to a theater near you. *(The OFFICERS, DR. HERMAN, BOBBY, and SUZIE run ON RIGHT, cross LEFT in terror, and EXIT LEFT as the giant AMOEBA [composed of unlimited EXTRAS, arms waving and undulating] ENTERS RIGHT, moves across the stage after them, and EXITS LEFT. The NARRATOR observes this and runs OFF RIGHT.)*

· · · · · · ·

11. There's No Place Like Home

RUNNING TIME: 7 minutes

CAST SIZE: 2M, 2F, 1E

CAST OF CHARACTERS

BETA-3...........................family's robot assistant

DR. ROBBINS.................father and head scientist on the Centurion 6 Spaceship

LILA ROBBINS.................overly dramatic sixteen-year-old daughter

MRS. ROBBINS...............perpetually cheerful wife; mother of the two children

BUDDY ROBBINS.............energetic and curious ten-year-old son

SETTING

TIME: The future.

PLACE: A deserted, unknown planet.

PROPERTIES

Cell phone.

THERE'S NO PLACE LIKE HOME

· · · · · · ·

BETA-3: *(ENTERS RIGHT, takes some robotic readings by holding up a finger as if to test the wind, and then calls to the OTHERS.)* I have done the necessary tests. This planet's environment is capable of sustaining human life. You can all come out of the spaceship and breathe normally. *(DR. ROBBINS, MRS. ROBBINS, LILA, and BUDDY stumble ON RIGHT, shaken up from their crash-landing. They look around the planet with caution.)*

DR. ROBBINS: *(Holds a small instrument shaped like a cell phone to take measurements.)* Beta-3 has correctly assessed the atmosphere. It is rich with oxygen. But proceed with caution, everyone. This planet is unknown to us. Danger could be lurking around any corner.

LILA: What happened, Dad? What went wrong? I thought we were supposed to land on planet Alpha Gamma Delta to begin a new human colony.

BETA-3: According to the ship's log, we were blasted by a barrage of meteors and thrown off course somewhere near the Nebulous Galaxy. Of course, you didn't notice anything because you were all frozen solid. I was rattled around like a bean in a maraca.

MRS. ROBBINS: Being suspended in a frozen state was the only way we could survive the tremendous time span required to travel to a distant galaxy.

BUDDY: *(Rubs his arms to warm up a little.)* All I know is it sure was cold. I still feel a little stiff.

MRS. ROBBINS: *(Smiles.)* Oh, Buddy, the stiffness will wear off soon. At least we're together and we're safe. *(Puts her arms around him.)*

DR. ROBBINS: Yes, for now. But where are we?

BETA-3: According to the data I have gathered from the ship's battered log, we are in the Quargon Galaxy on an uncharted planet.

DR. ROBBINS: *(Looks around.)* The Quargon Galaxy? That doesn't sound good. The landscape is comprised of jagged rock formations and coarse, dry sand.

BETA-3: It does not appear to be a very hospitable environment, Dr. Robbins.

LILA: Wait just a minute, Daddy! You promised me that we were going to a beautiful planet with lush gardens and waterfalls. You said we would be the first family to start building the colony and that millions of other families would be joining us soon, so I would have lots of friends. That's the only reason I agreed to come along on this ridiculous adventure. No way am I going to be stuck in this ugly place for the rest of my life. Let's go back to the ship, start up the jet engines, and high-tail it out of here back to Earth!

BUDDY: Aw, come on, sis. This planet is cool, and just think! We may be the first humans to set foot on it! You never know what we might find here. Maybe some giant space trolls or alien life forms. Come on, let's go exploring! *(Starts to run OFF LEFT.)*

MRS. ROBBINS: *(Grabs him. Smiles widely, as always.)* Hold on there, tiger! We need to stay together for now. Maybe you can go exploring a little later, after your father has secured the area.

BUDDY: *(Disappointed and exaggerated.)* Aw, Mom!

DR. ROBBINS: Your mother's right, Buddy. We need to stick together. And Lila, don't worry. Someday we will get to Alpha Gamma Delta and start that colony, but it's going to take some time for Beta-3 and me to fix the ship. The meteors did a lot of damage to the engines. In the meantime, we need to set up a safe homestead for ourselves. We may be here awhile. We might as well make the best of it. *(EXITS RIGHT with BETA-3.)*

MRS. ROBBINS: Don't look so glum, Lila. Think of this as an adventure.

LILA: Some adventure. I'm stuck on a deserted planet with my mom, dad, little brother, and a robot. Whoopee! It reminds me of our vacation to the Grand Canyon last summer. That was the worst week of my life—until now!

MRS. ROBBINS: *(Cheery.)* Oh, come on, Lila. Turn that frown upside down! Remember, attitude is everything. And for your information, young lady, I loved that trip to the Grand Canyon. A whole week with my three favorite people! What could be better? *(Puts her arms around LILA and BUDDY and gives them a hug.)* We'll get through this, you'll see, because we have each other!

LILA: Oh, Mother. Really? Don't you ever get upset about anything? Look around this planet. Just rocks, gravel, and sand! There's absolutely nothing to be happy about. We're no place!

BUDDY: *(Excited.)* We may be no place, but I think this planet looks awesome. *(Points OFF LEFT.)* Can I please go climb those rock formations, Mom? Maybe I can see some aliens or something.

MRS. ROBBINS: Okay, if you're careful. And remember, Buddy, if you do see any unusual life forms, *they* aren't the aliens, *you* are!

BUDDY: *(Laughs.)* That's right. I'll keep that in mind, I promise. *(Runs OFF LEFT.)*

MRS. ROBBINS: *(Waves after him.)* Don't go too far, young man!

BETA-3: *(ENTERS RIGHT with DR. ROBBINS.)* The ship's in pretty bad shape, Doctor. It's going to take some time to get it up and running again. We have no communication capability and only enough food and water for sixty days. I don't think mission control will ever think to look for us here in the Quargon Galaxy.

DR. ROBBINS: We had better do some exploring and see if this planet can provide any resources.

BETA-3: According to my calculations, a planet this size with an oxygen-rich environment must have a water source. If there is water and oxygen, life forms are likely to exist. Shall I begin mapping the most probable locations to search, Doctor?

DR. ROBBINS: Yes, Beta-3. You start computing, and I will work on the communications system. Mrs. Robbins and Lila can start setting up a homestead and boil some packets of food for dinner. Buddy, you come with me and help... *(Looks around for BUDDY.)* Where's Buddy? Where did he go? *(Calls out.)* Buddy? Buddy!

MRS. ROBBINS: I let him go exploring, dear. He said he wouldn't go far.

DR. ROBBINS: You let him go exploring? What were you thinking? We have no idea what might be lurking out there in those rock formations.

MRS. ROBBINS: *(No longer smiling.)* Oh, dear. Poor Buddy!

DR. ROBBINS: I've got to find him before it's too late.

MRS. ROBBINS: I'll go with you!

LILA: I'm coming, too!

BETA-3: I will accompany you, as well! *(DR. ROBBINS, MRS. ROBBINS, BETA-3, and LILA start to EXIT LEFT. BUDDY ENTERS LEFT.)*

DR. ROBBINS: Buddy! Are you all right, son?

MRS. ROBBINS: Oh, Buddy! We were so worried. I never should have let you go off by yourself.

LILA: *(Messes up his hair affectionately.)* Aw, I knew you'd be okay, little brother.

BUDDY: *(Bubbles with excitement.)* I'm fine, everybody. Really! I was just doing some exploring. I climbed to the top of that huge rock wall over there, and guess what I saw on the other side?

DR. ROBBINS: What, son?

BUDDY: Beautiful tropical gardens and a huge waterfall. There are animals running all over the place and rainbows and unicorns. Come on, I'll show you!

DR. ROBBINS: Do you know what this means, Beta-3? The ship's calculations were way off. The meteor barrage didn't cause us to land on a barren, uncharted planet in the Quargon Galaxy. We have landed on Alpha Gamma Delta, after all.

BUDDY: That's right, Dad. We made it!

MRS. ROBBINS: *(Smiles again.)* It's a miracle! We made it! We can build the colony, and soon we will welcome millions of other Earth families.

LILA: What a relief!

DR. ROBBINS: I knew we'd make it. I just knew it. Beta-3, prepare to launch an exploration party. Buddy, you stick with me. Mrs. Robbins and Lila, you pack some provisions for our journey.

LILA: Why do Mom and I always have to do the girl stuff? I want to go exploring, too.

DR. ROBBINS: There will be plenty of time for that, Lila. *(Puts his arms around his family, and they face the AUDIENCE as if in a portrait.)* Just think of it. We are the first Earth family to live on Alpha Gamma Delta—our new home! And you know what they say...

ALL: *(Together, happy.)* There's no place like home!

· · · · · · ·

12. What Kind of Ghoul Am I?

RUNNING TIME: 7 minutes

CAST SIZE: 1M, 1F

CAST OF CHARACTERS

MR. GHOUL ....vampire trying to hide
his identity; has heavy
Transylvanian accent

MRS. GHOUL ....Mr. Ghoul's devoted spouse; no
distinct accent

SETTING

The house of the Ghouls.

PROPERTIES

Two chairs, coffee table, book, cape, hat, pajamas, robe.

What Kind of Ghoul Am I?

· · · · · · ·

Two chairs and a coffee table with a book on it are set up CENTER. It is midnight. MR. GHOUL ENTERS LEFT, trying to be extremely quiet. He puts on a cape and a hat and tiptoes RIGHT. MRS. GHOUL ENTERS LEFT in her pajamas and robe.

MRS. GHOUL: *(Yawns a big yawn and stretches her arms.)* Ahhhh! *(Notices MR. GHOUL.)* Harold? Harold, what are you doing? Are you going somewhere?

MR. GHOUL: *(Acts nonchalant.)* Oh, my dear! What are you doing up at this time of night?

MRS. GHOUL: *(Suspicious.)* I might ask you the same question. Were you going somewhere, my dear?

MR. GHOUL: I just couldn't sleep, that's all. I thought I'd go out for a little stroll. *(Tries to usher her OFF LEFT.)* Why don't you go back to bed, my dear, and I'll see you in the morning.

MRS. GHOUL: You have certainly had a lot of trouble sleeping lately. Maybe you should see a doctor.

MR. GHOUL: I'm sure it's nothing, my dear. I'm just a bit of a night owl, that's all. Now go to bed. You don't want to miss your beauty sleep.

MRS. GHOUL: Maybe I'll have a cup of warm milk before I go back to bed. *(Starts to head OFF RIGHT.)*

MR. GHOUL: *(Stops her and tries to move her back OFF LEFT.)* As a matter of fact, I think we're all out of milk. Let me just run down to the corner store and pick some up for you. I know how a glass of warm milk helps you sleep. You stay here, and I'll be right back. *(Starts OFF RIGHT again.)*

MRS. GHOUL: Dear, it's after midnight. The corner store closes at nine o'clock. *(MR. GHOUL snaps his fingers out of his wife's view, as if to say, "Darn it!")* I guess we'll just have to go to sleep and get some milk in the morning.

MR. GHOUL: You go to sleep, dear. I'm just going to watch a little TV before I turn in.

MRS. GHOUL: Don't be ridiculous. There's nothing on the television this late.

MR. GHOUL: Then I'll read for a while. You go count some sheep, and I will stay out here and read. Good night! *(Picks up the book and sits on a chair.)*

MRS. GHOUL: *(Hesitant.)* Well, okay. If you insist. I'll just go back to bed. Don't stay up too late. *(EXITS LEFT. MR. GHOUL listens to make sure she's gone, then puts his book down and sneaks RIGHT again. MRS. GHOUL RE-ENTERS LEFT.)* I just want to get a glass of water before... *(Sees MR. GHOUL almost OFF RIGHT and is a little miffed.)* Where are you going?

MR. GHOUL: *(Startled.)* Oh, my dear! You frightened me! I just heard something howling out in the front yard and thought I'd go investigate. *(MRS. GHOUL stands with her arms crossed, disbelieving.)* It sounded like a vicious monster or a zombie or a giant werewolf or something like that. It was a blood-curdling howl. *(Imitates the howl.)* Don't be frightened, my dear! I will protect you, but I must go check it out. You stay right here. I should be back in an hour or so. *(Starts OFF RIGHT again.)*

MRS. GHOUL: *(Gets mad.)* Wait a minute, buster. I didn't hear anything howling in the front yard. What are you really up to? Come on. It's about time you tell me the truth!

MR. GHOUL: *(Finally gives up, but takes his time with the confession.)* All right, my dear. If you want to know the truth, I will tell you the truth. You had better sit down. *(Ushers MRS. GHOUL to a chair.)* I don't want you to be frightened, my dear. You know I would never hurt you.

MRS. GHOUL: Of course.

MR. GHOUL: I have a little secret I've been keeping from you since we were married.

MRS. GHOUL: Since we were married? But we've been married for twenty-five years!

MR. GHOUL: I know. Believe me, it hasn't been easy.

MRS. GHOUL: Well, go ahead and tell me. What is this deep, dark secret of yours?

MR. GHOUL: *(Takes a deep breath and states slowly.)* I... am... a vampire. There. I said it, finally. I am a vampire! Oh, my. I feel so liberated! *(Stands and starts dancing around.)* I am a vampire! I am a vampire!

MRS. GHOUL: *(Shocked.)* What are you saying? Do you mean to tell me that you're one of those people who go around biting necks and drinking human blood? That's ridiculous!

MR. GHOUL: Yes, my dear. That's exactly what I mean. I love the taste of human blood! I can't survive without it! That's why I must go out every night to find my victims. *(Laughs diabolically.)*

MRS. GHOUL: Well, that can't be good. What happens to your victims after you drink their blood?

MR. GHOUL: Oh, they're fine. It doesn't really hurt them. They just turn into zombie-like creatures and go about their day.

MRS. GHOUL: They turn into zombie-like creatures? *(Considers this.)* Wait a minute. It's all making sense to me now. So you mean... *(Thinks a moment.)* ...Mrs. Harrison, the Avon lady?

MR. GHOUL: That was very convenient. She came to me. Ding-dong, Avon calling. *(Marks an imaginary scoreboard in the air with his finger.)* Victim!

MRS. GHOUL: And the Taylor twins who came to the house selling Girl Scout cookies?

MR. GHOUL: *(Licks his lips.)* Mmm. I love those Tagalongs. *(Marks two more strokes in the air.)* Victim, victim.

MRS. GHOUL: And Rusty Fenton, the paperboy?

MR. GHOUL: *(Remembers.)* Oh, yes! He came a little too early one morning, missed the porch again, and well... victim!

MRS. GHOUL: I thought our neighbors have been looking a little fatigued lately.

MR. GHOUL: Anemic is more like it, my dear.

MRS. GHOUL: So what else are you hiding? Is that it? Are there any more terrible secrets you've been keeping from me?

MR. GHOUL: I may have fudged on my age a bit.

MRS. GHOUL: Your age? Why? How old are you?

MR. GHOUL: *(Hesitates.)* Seven hundred years old, give or take a few decades.

MRS. GHOUL: *(Shocked again.)* What? Seven hundred years old? But we just threw a big party for your fiftieth birthday!

MR. GHOUL: Yes, well, sorry about that.

MRS. GHOUL: *(Upset.)* So I don't suppose this is your first marriage, either.

MR. GHOUL: Um, maybe not.

MRS. GHOUL: Maybe not?

MR. GHOUL: I vaguely recall a few others.

MRS. GHOUL: A few others? How many others?

MR. GHOUL: Only forty or so. Not that many, really.

MRS. GHOUL: Forty marriages? I don't know what to say. It all makes sense to me now. I understand why you would never eat my Chicken Fettuccini.

MR. GHOUL: I can't stand the garlic.

MRS. GHOUL: And why you would never smile in any of our family pictures.

MR. GHOUL: I don't like to show off my fangs.

MRS. GHOUL: And why you prefer sleeping in that wooden coffin instead of a cozy, comfy bed.

MR. GHOUL: I do have a bad back.

MRS. GHOUL: I must say, I'm glad you finally told me. What a relief! I was afraid you were sneaking out at night because you don't love me anymore. *(Starts to whimper.)*

MR. GHOUL: *(Comforts her.)* Oh, my darling! Don't be ridiculous! You are my joy, my essence, my reason for living!

MRS. GHOUL: *(Sniffles.)* Really?

MR. GHOUL: Of course! Would I lie to you? Now you go back to sleep, and I'll be home shortly. I just want to have a little nightcap with the guys.

MRS. GHOUL: Okay. I guess I'll go back to bed. *(Starts OFF LEFT then turns back.)* Oh, one more question, dear... my mother?

MR. GHOUL: *(Laughs maniacally.)* Victim!

• • • • • • •

13. Super-Duper Heroes

RUNNING TIME: 6 minutes

CAST SIZE: 2M, 2F

CAST OF CHARACTERS

UMBRELLA GIRL .... can expand her body into an umbrella shape

LADDER MAN .... able to stretch his body for thousands of feet

DUCT TAPE WOMAN .... gets very creative with duct tape

SNACK BOY .... specializes in providing snacks

SETTING

The secret hideout of Umbrella Girl.

PROPERTIES

Two cell phones, many rolls of duct tape in various colors and patterns, three bags.

Super-Duper Heroes

. . . .

UMBRELLA GIRL: *(Stands CENTER; speaks into a cell phone.)* Yes, Madam President. I understand the urgency of the situation. There is a meteor the size of the Rhode Island hurtling toward Earth at this very moment. That does sound serious, Madam President. You've come to the right superhero, ma'am. I will contact my colleagues at once. Don't worry, Madam President. We will not fail the people of Earth. We will figure out a way to stop that meteor before it's too late! Good-bye, Madam President. *(Hangs up.)* Hm. Let's see... a giant meteor hurtling toward Earth at the speed of light. I must figure out a way to stop the giant destroyer before it's too late. One thing I do know—I can't do this alone. *(Scrolls through the contacts on her phone.)* What superpowers do I need to help in this dire situation? Hammer Man? No, not Hammer Man. What about Spelling Girl? No, I don't think her tremendous vocabulary and perfect grammar will help in this situation. Pumpkin Boy? Pole Vault Woman? All amazing superheroes, but I need just the right team to help with this looming catastrophe. *(Has an idea.)* I've got it! *(Speaks into the phone.)* Siri? Get me Ladder Man immediately. It's a matter of international security. *(Waits a few seconds.)* Ladder Man? This is Umbrella Girl. We have an emergency on our hands. Can you rush right over to my secret hideout? Thanks!

LADDER MAN: *(ENTERS RIGHT.)* I came as fast as I could, Umbrella Girl. What's the emergency?

UMBRELLA GIRL: Ladder Man, thanks for coming. I need your help. I just spoke to the president, and she has informed me that there is a giant meteor the size of Rhode Island hurtling toward Earth at the speed of light. It's headed for South America, and when it hits, Earth as we know it will cease to exist.

LADDER MAN: *(Shocked.)* Holy disaster, Umbrella Girl! This is serious!

UMBRELLA GIRL: The world needs our help, Ladder Man, and I have come up with a plan! But it's going to take a group effort. *(Paces.)* I am certain I can morph my body into a large enough umbrella to spread across South America, but I need your super extension skills to get me as high into the atmosphere as possible. When the meteor hits my elastic body, it will be slung back into the galaxy, saving the people of Earth from certain disaster.

LADDER MAN: Brilliant, Umbrella Girl. I am confident I can extend my ladder-shaped body high into the atmosphere, lifting your umbrella-shaped body as far as the ozone layer, if necessary.

UMBRELLA GIRL: Excellent! But I foresee a problem. I don't believe I will be able to hold on to you at that extreme altitude and not fly away. We must somehow secure my arm to your extension ladder. *(Paces around the stage with LADDER MAN as they think.)*

LADDER MAN: I've got it! We need Duct Tape Woman!

UMBRELLA GIRL: Duct Tape Woman?

LADDER MAN: Of course! Duct Tape Woman can make anything stick together. She can adhere one of your arms to my head so that you won't fly away. I worked with her on a potential building collapse last month. She had that structure secured and sound in no time. The building is still standing to this day. She also gives you your choice of colors and patterns.

UMBRELLA GIRL: That sounds like the answer, Ladder Man! Quick! Give her a call!

LADDER MAN: *(Pulls out his cell phone; urgent.)* Siri? Get me Duct Tape Woman immediately. This is an emergency!

(Waits a couple seconds.) Duct Tape Woman? This is Ladder Man. We have an emergency. Can you come to Umbrella Girl's hideout right away? And bring all the duct tape you've got! *(Puts away the cell phone.)*

DUCT TAPE WOMAN: *(Rushes ON RIGHT with a large bag.)* I got here ASAP! What's the emergency, Ladder Man?

LADDER MAN: The President of the United States has asked for help. There is a giant meteor the size of the Rhode Island hurtling toward South America at the speed of light. If this wayward giant hits the earth, mankind is doomed! Umbrella Girl has come up with a plan, but she needs our help!

DUCT TAPE WOMAN: What's the ETA?

UMBRELLA GIRL: Ten p.m. PST.

LADDER MAN: *(To DUCT TAPE WOMAN.)* Did you BYOT?

DUCT TAPE WOMAN: *(Pulls rolls of duct tape in various colors and patterns out of her bag.)* I always bring my own tape, Ladder Man. BTW, Umbrella Girl, what's your plan?

UMBRELLA GIRL: Well, the wayward giant—AKA the meteor—is hurtling toward S.A. We need to deflect it back into space. My plan is to climb up Ladder Man, who will extend his body into the ozone layer. Then I will morph my body into a giant, flexible umbrella.

DUCT TAPE WOMAN: *(Laughs hysterically.)* LOL! That will be a sight to see! Where do I come in?

LADDER MAN: We need you to climb up after Umbrella Girl and duct tape her arm to my head so she won't fly away like a huge parachute. Once her arm is secured, she will aim her body toward the oncoming meteor and deflect it back into space, thereby saving Earth from destruction.

DUCT TAPE WOMAN: Brilliant plan, Umbrella Girl! Count me in! I see only one little problem with your plan.

UMBRELLA GIRL: What is that, Duct Tape Woman?

DUCT TAPE WOMAN: The job will be long and difficult. We're going to need provisions.

UMBRELLA GIRL: Of course! Provisions! Why didn't I think of this before?

LADDER MAN: I've got it! I'll call Snack Boy right away!

DUCT TAPE WOMAN: Brilliant idea, Ladder Man. But tell him to hurry. We haven't much time to spare.

LADDER MAN: *(Takes out his cell phone.)* Siri? Get me Snack Boy immediately! It's a matter of international security! *(Waits a few seconds.)* Snack Boy? This is Ladder Man. I have Umbrella Girl and Duct Tape Woman here with me at Umbrella Girl's hideout. We need your superhero help. There's a giant meteor the size of the Rhode Island hurtling toward South America at the speed of light. Can you get here ASAP? Thanks! *(Puts his cell phone away.)*

SNACK BOY: *(Rushes ON RIGHT, holding a bag in each arm. In a sing-song manner.)* Who needs a snack?

UMBRELLA GIRL: What took you so long, Snack Boy? We've got a meteor to stop and no time to lose! Now, do we have everything we need?

SNACK BOY: I brought pretzels, carrots, and juice boxes. Will that be enough?

UMBRELLA GIRL: That should hold us over until we get back. Good job, Snack Boy!

LADDER MAN: I brought my extra stretchy spandex so I can extend my body as far as possible into the atmosphere.

UMBRELLA GIRL: Good thinking, Ladder Man. Way to plan ahead!

DUCT TAPE WOMAN: I brought a colorful assortment of duct tape in solids and patterns for any eventuality. We won't be lacking in adhesive power.

UMBRELLA GIRL: Outstanding, Duct Tape Woman. Smart and trendy at the same time!

SNACK BOY: I also brought some sunscreen, just in case. You can never be too careful when it comes to sun exposure!

UMBRELLA GIRL: Brilliant, Snack Boy! Why didn't I think of that? Well, I guess we better fly. I can't thank you enough for all your help. People may never know the importance of our mission, but we will know that we have saved the world from certain destruction. *(SUPERHEROES gather in a semi-circle huddle facing the AUDIENCE and put their hands in the middle for a final cheer.)*

LADDER MAN: South America, here we come!

ALL: Let's go! *(They break out of the huddle and EXIT RIGHT)*

· · · · · · ·

14. That Old Silk Hat

RUNNING TIME: 8 minutes

CAST SIZE: 3M, 2F, 1E

CAST OF CHARACTERS

NARRATOR......................Rod Serling-type character with
a dramatic flair

KAREN ....lively young girl

SANDRA ....bright, friendly girl

CARL..............................fun-loving boy

SAMMY ....shy but adventurous boy

CHILLY...........................very mysterious but happy
snowman

SETTING

TIME: The mid-sixties.

PLACE: The Twilight Realm. A snow-covered street in a small town.

PROPERTIES

Four pairs of mittens, four scarves, four coats, old top hat, corncob pipe.

That Old Silk Hat

· · · · · · ·

NARRATOR: *(ENTERS LEFT and steps forward.)* Time—the mid-sixties. Place—the northernmost section of the Northeastern United States. The air is icy and cold. The little town is blanketed in a coat of frosty white—a storybook setting for a lovely winter's day. Today we will witness a common children's game of hide-and-go-seek as it is innocently played on a snow-drifted lane. But look beyond the innocence of childish play for something lost is soon to be found—here, in the Twilight Realm. *(Steps back.)*

KAREN: *(Runs ON RIGHT with SANDRA and looks around the stage anxiously. They are dressed in mittens, scarves, and coats.)* Come on, Sandra. We can hide over there behind that big drift of snow.

SANDRA: Good idea, Karen. The boys will never find us there. *(GIRLS run OFF LEFT.)*

SAMMY: *(Runs ON RIGHT with CARL, also dressed in mittens, scarves, and coats. They look around the stage.)* They must be around here someplace, Carl.

CARL: Maybe they're hiding behind that thicket over there. Come on. Let's go! *(BOYS run OFF RIGHT. GIRLS run ON LEFT. KAREN is holding an old top hat.)*

SANDRA: Where do you think it came from?

KAREN: I have no idea. It was just laying in the snow drift. Maybe someone lost it.

SANDRA: Or maybe someone was trying to get rid of it.

KAREN: We better call the boys and see what they think. *(Calls out.)* Olly-olly-oxen-free! Olly-olly-oxen-free! *(BOYS run ON RIGHT.)*

CARL: You gave up already? We would have found you in a couple more minutes.

SANDRA: Don't be silly. We didn't give up. We found something we thought you should see.

KAREN: *(Holds out the hat.)* Look at this! *(BOYS examine the hat closely.)*

SAMMY: So what? It's just an old hat.

CARL: Yeah. It's just a dirty old hat. You stopped the game for that?

KAREN: It's not just a dirty old hat. *(Rubs the top of the hat.)* I have a feeling this hat is special.

CARL: Well, what are you gonna do with it? *(Reaches for it.)* Can I try it on?

KAREN: *(Pulls it away.)* Absolutely not! You'll ruin it!

SANDRA: Hey, I know! Why don't we build a snowman? A great big snowman! Then we can dress him up and put the hat on his head.

KAREN: Great idea, Sandra! He'll be the most dashing snowman in the whole town.

SAMMY: Can Carl and I help?

KAREN: Sure! Let's get to work! *(CHILDREN pantomime building a snowman. CHILLY sneaks ON RIGHT, hidden from the audience by the CHILDREN, and FREEZES UP CENTER.)*

NARRATOR: *(Steps forward as the CHILDREN work and speaks slowly and with mystery.)* So the children build a snowman—how sweet. What a delightful winter pastime. They build him solid and strong, packing the ice and snow with their mittened hands. They give him a corncob pipe, a button nose, and two eyes made out of a couple of rocks they found lying around. Sandra wraps her warm scarf around the snowman's neck. He is almost finished except for that old silk hat they found. *(Steps back as the CHILDREN open up to reveal CHILLY, standing rigidly and staring out toward the AUDIENCE.)*

KAREN: He looks terrific! Good work, everybody! And now for the final touch. *(Slowly places the hat on CHILLY'S head as the OTHER CHILDREN look on with excitement.)* There! *(Steps back to admire him.)* Have you ever seen a more elegant snowman? I think that hat was made just for him.

CHILLY: *(His right arm starts to tremble, then his left arm starts to tremble, next his right leg, then his left leg. Pretty soon, his entire body is shaking. He stops suddenly, looks forward, and speaks loudly.)* Happy Hanukkah! *(CHILDREN are speechless.)* Not Happy Hanukkah? Then Happy Kwanzaa!

CARL: *(Frightened.)* Wha... what's happening? Did he just say something?

SAMMY: *(Scared.)* It can't be true! Snowmen don't talk.

CHILLY: They don't? But *I* seem to be talking.

SANDRA: *(Starts to take slow steps backward in a loud whisper.)* Everybody just step away from the scary snowman. *(CHILDREN start to step back with slow steps.)*

CHILLY: *(Doesn't quite understand and starts to step backward, too. Also in a loud whisper.)* Why are we doing this?

SAMMY: Everybody get ready to run. Ready? One, two, three, run! *(The CHILDREN panic and run in different directions. CHILLY runs in panic, too, though not sure what they're running from. In the confusion, CHILLY'S hat is knocked from his head, and he FREEZES. The CHILDREN stop and look at him.)*

KAREN: What happened? He's frozen again.

SANDRA: This is really creepy.

CARL: Sandra's right. Let's get out of here before he wakes up again. *(Starts to run OFF RIGHT.)*

SAMMY: I'm right behind you, Carl. *(Follows CARL.)*

KAREN: Wait a minute! *(Picks up the hat and examines it as the BOYS turn back.)* When did the snowman come to life?

SANDRA: As soon as we gave him that corncob pipe.

CARL: No, it was as soon as Sandra gave him that button nose.

SAMMY: No, you're both wrong. He came to life as soon as I gave him those two eyes made out of a couple of rocks I found lying around.

KAREN: I think you're all remembering it wrong. He didn't come to life until I put this old silk hat on his head. Remember?

CARL/SAMMY/SANDRA: *(Together.)* Oh, yeah! *(KAREN holds out the top hat as the CHILDREN look at it closer.)*

CARL: Do you think that hat's got magic powers?

SAMMY: Maybe there's a curse on it.

KAREN: Maybe it's from outer space.

SANDRA: Maybe it's bewitched.

CARL: What are we going to do with it?

SAMMY: Get rid of it!

SANDRA: No, wait. Maybe we'd better test it just one more time.

CARL: No way! I'm getting out of here!

KAREN: Oh, come on. Just one more time. We'll put it on the snowman's head, and everybody be ready to run.

SANDRA: I'm with you, Karen. Go ahead. He actually seemed like a pretty friendly snowman, though we only knew him for a few seconds. I mean, he even wished us a happy Hanukkah!

KAREN: You're right, Sandra. He was pretty nice and very polite, and we did sort of scare him with our screaming. Let's give it another try. Maybe he would play with us.

SANDRA: Yeah! We could march around town with our very own live snowman. Wouldn't that be fun?

SAMMY: I don't know. I think we should quit while we're ahead.

CARL: Me, too!

KAREN: You boys worry too much! He's just a friendly snowman and we're the lucky kids who get to play with him!

SAMMY: Well, okay. If you think it's safe.

CARL: Maybe just one more try.

KAREN: Good. Now I'm going to place the magic hat on his head, and we'll see what happens. *(Slowly approaches CHILLY.)*

SANDRA: Can you imagine what the kids at school will say when we tell them about our living snowman?

CARL: You're right. They'll be so jealous! *(KAREN places the hat on CHILLY'S head once again.)*

CHILLY: *(Goes through the same shaking process and comes to life again, cheerful.)* Happy Hanukkah!

ALL CHILDREN: *(Together, excited.)* Happy Hanukkah, Mr. Snowman!

CHILLY: You can call me Chilly. That's my name!

ALL CHILDREN: Happy Hanukkah, Chilly!

CHILLY: Let's play "Follow the Leader!"

ALL CHILDREN: That sounds great, Chilly! *(They follow CHILLY as they form a line and march around the stage. They march happily for a few seconds, and then CHILLY begins to wobble. He goes to his knees and marches for a time in this position.)* Hey, what's going on? I seem to be shorter than when we started.

KAREN: Oh, no. It's starting to warm up. Chilly's melting!

SANDRA: Oh, no! Poor Chilly.

CARL: Ugh! He's liquefying. Gross!

SAMMY: I can't look!

CHILLY: *(Slowly melts, reminiscent of the Wicked Witch of the West.)* I'm melting. Melting! Ahhh! *(Collapses to the floor. CHILDREN stand around him, very sad.)*

KAREN: Poor Chilly. All that's left is his old, silk hat.

CARL: That was the saddest thing I've ever seen.

SAMMY: I'll never build another snowman again in my life.

KAREN: Chilly was the best snowman ever!

CARL: Yeah. The best ever.

SANDRA: What should we do with the hat now? *(CHILDREN think for a moment.)*

KAREN: I'm going to keep it, and the next time it snows, we can build a new Chilly!

SANDRA: That's a great idea. We'll just have to wait until it gets cold again.

KAREN: Don't worry, Chilly. We'll be back. We'll bring you to life again. *(The CHILDREN walk away sadly.)*

NARRATOR: *(Steps forward.)* So sad, a cruel twist of fate. A liquefied snowman and four shattered children. There's an old saying that goes, "If the shoe fits, wear it." But be forewarned—if you happen to find an old silk hat lying in a snow drift, be careful before you put it on your snowman. You might have to give a nod to... *(Pantomimes tipping a hat.)* ...the Twilight Realm.

. . . .

15. Heckle or Jekyll?

RUNNING TIME: 9 minutes

CAST SIZE: 4M, 2F

CAST OF CHARACTERS

MRS. REARDON ....jovial housekeeper for Dr. Jekyll
CONSTABLE ....local officer who is all business
MISS SAUNDERS ....worried neighbor; missing her
dog
MR. FLETCHER...............another anxious neighbor;
missing his wife
DR. JEKYLL...................unfriendly and secretive doctor
MR. HECKLE ....evil counterpart to Dr. Jekyll

SETTING

Dr. Jekyll's lovely English home.

PROPERTIES

Two nice chairs, coffee table, door, window, notebook, tray,
pot of tea, plate of scones, napkins.

SOUND EFFECT

Doorbell.

Heckle or Jekyll?

. . . .

There are two nice chairs and a coffee table at CENTER, along with a door and a window UP LEFT (NOTE: Door and window can be pantomimed). MR. HECKLE is ONSTAGE, hiding behind one of the chairs. SOUND EFFECT: DOORBELL RINGS.

MRS. REARDON: *(ENTERS RIGHT. Cheerful, in a sing-song manner.)* I'll get it! *(Goes to the door and opens it.)* Good day, Constable. What a lovely surprise! Won't you come in? *(CONSTABLE, MISS SAUNDERS, and MR. FLETCHER ENTER UP LEFT through the door. MISS SAUNDERS and MR. FLETCHER look around cautiously, frightened.)* Can I interest you in a cup of tea and some scones? They are fresh from the oven. Dr. Jekyll just loves his morning scone, you see, and it is my duty to see that they are always fresh and ready for tea. Won't you sit down?

CONSTABLE: We are not here for tea, Mrs. Reardon. We are here on official police business.

MRS. REARDON: Oh, dear. That does sound serious. Is Dr. Jekyll expecting you?

CONSTABLE: I don't imagine so, Mrs. Reardon. *(Gestures to the OTHERS.)* You know Miss Saunders and Mr. Fletcher, I presume?

MRS. REARDON: Of course I do. We've been neighbors for many years. How is your lovely little dog, Miss Saunders?

MISS SAUNDERS: *(Tearful.)* Missing, I'm afraid.

MRS. REARDON: Oh, dear. I am distressed to hear that. And Mr. Fletcher, how is your lovely wife, Anna?

MR. FLETCHER: *(Tearful.)* Also missing. I haven't seen her for a week.

CONSTABLE: That's why we are here, Mrs. Reardon. There have been reports of some strange things going on in and around Dr. Jekyll's home, and we want to talk with him.

MRS. REARDON: I am sure he will be happy to talk with you. He loves welcoming company. Of course, I am just his housekeeper, so I don't imagine I can be of much help. Let me call the doctor for you, Constable.

CONSTABLE: Thank you, Mrs. Reardon. I would appreciate that.

MRS. REARDON: *(Crosses RIGHT and calls out in a sing-song manner.)* Dr. Jekyll? You have visitors. Can you come up here, please? *(To CONSTABLE.)* He'll be here in just a moment, Constable. He's been spending a lot of time in his laboratory lately. He just loves his little experiments. I have no idea what he's working on. He won't let me near his laboratory—not even to clean! Are you sure you wouldn't like some tea?

DR. JEKYLL: *(ENTERS RIGHT, irritable.)* If it isn't the Constable. What a delightful surprise. And Miss Saunders and Mr. Fletcher, what an unexpected pleasure. What brings you to my humble home this fine morning? Won't you sit down?

CONSTABLE: No, thank you, Dr. Jekyll. I would rather stand, if you don't mind. We are here on official business.

DR. JEKYLL: *(Appears cool and calm.)* Official business? That sounds quite ominous. Mrs. Reardon, are those scones ready yet?

MRS. REARDON: Yes, sir. I'll get them right away, sir. *(EXITS RIGHT.)*

DR. JEKYLL: Mrs. Reardon makes the most delicious scones, you know. I must have at least one every morning. *(Sits casually.)* Now, Constable, how can I be of service?

CONSTABLE: *(Pulls out a notebook.)* Well, Dr. Jekyll, we've received several reports of strange happenings in your neighborhood, and I am wondering if you could shed some light on any of these incidents.

DR. JEKYLL: *(Becomes noticeably agitated and tries to control himself.)* Of course, Constable. I am glad to help in any way I can. We certainly want our neighborhood to be safe, don't we? What can I do?

CONSTABLE: *(Refers to his notes.)* It appears that several of your neighbors and local pets have gone missing in recent months.

DR. JEKYLL: No! That's dreadful! What do you think is happening to them, Constable?

CONSTABLE: If I knew, I wouldn't be here, would I?

DR. JEKYLL: *(Chuckles)* Of course not. Please, go on.

MISS SAUNDERS: *(Gains the courage to speak.)* I am missing my little dog, Muffy, Dr. Jekyll, and I have seen a strange man coming and going from your house lately. A very evil-looking man.

DR. JEKYLL: *(Starts to twitch and shake.)* An evil-looking man, you say? Coming out of my house? Impossible, Miss Saunders. *(Unable to control himself any longer, points at the window to divert their attention.)* Look out the window! I believe it's your little dog! *(As OTHERS look, DR. JEKYLL DISAPPEARS behind the chair, and MR. HECKLE EMERGES. OTHERS look back and are startled.)*

CONSTABLE: Who are you? Where did Dr. Jekyll go?

MR. HECKLE: Dr. Jekyll had some sudden business to attend to, but he told me to tell you that he would be right back. Brilliant man, that Dr. Jekyll. Absolutely brilliant. I'm Mr. Heckle. I stop in every morning for a scone or two. How can I help you?

CONSTABLE: *(Suspicious.)* Mr. Heckle, is it? *(Looks at MISS SAUNDERS and MR. FLETCHER, who are confused.)*

MR. HECKLE: *(Wrings his hands with an evil look.)* That's right, Constable. Mr. Heckle, at your service.

CONSTABLE: Mr. Heckle, we are here about the disappearance of Miss Saunders's little dog, Muffy—

MR. FLETCHER: *(Interrupts.)* And my wife, Anna.

CONSTABLE: Have you seen either of them recently?

MR. HECKLE: I don't know. Maybe I did, and maybe I didn't. There are lots of dogs around here, and ladies walk down this street every day. In fact, there's a lady walking by right now. *(Points to the window, and CONSTABLE, MISS SAUNDERS, and MR. FLETCHER turn to look. They stay facing away as MR. HECKLE DISAPPEARS behind the chair and DR. JEKYLL REAPPEARS. He walks up behind the OTHERS.)*

DR. JEKYLL: *(Calm and collected.)* What are you looking at? *(OTHERS turn suddenly, surprised, and gasp.)*

MR. FLETCHER: *(Stutters.)* Wh... Where did you come from?

MRS. REARDON: *(ENTERS RIGHT with a tray of tea and scones, cheerful.)* Here we are. Nice fresh scones and a pot of tea.

DR. JEKYLL: Wonderful, Mrs. Reardon! I'm famished. Would anyone else care for a scone? *(OTHERS are still shaken.)*

CONSTABLE: Where did he go?

DR. JEKYLL: *(Innocent.)* Where did who go?

CONSTABLE: That strange, sinister man who was just here—Mr. Heckle!

DR. JEKYLL: Mr. Heckle? Don't be absurd. I don't know anyone by the name of Mr. Heckle, do you, Mrs. Reardon?

MRS. REARDON: I don't think so, sir. *(Changes the subject.)* Can I pour out for everyone?

CONSTABLE: Now wait just a minute. There's something very strange going on around here.

MRS. REARDON: Oops! I forgot the napkins. I'll be right back. *(EXITS RIGHT.)*

CONSTABLE: I'm going to get to the bottom of this if it's the last thing I do!

DR. JEKYLL: *(Becomes agitated again, and his hands start to shake. Suddenly, he points to the window.)* Is that the evil man you were talking about? *(CONSTABLE, MISS SAUNDERS, and MR. FLETCHER look away again. DR. JEKYLL DISAPPEARS behind the chair again as MR. HECKLE REAPPEARS, runs to the window, grabs MISS SAUNDERS without the OTHERS noticing, and drags her OFF LEFT. There is a scuffle OFF LEFT as CONSTABLE and MR. FLETCHER continue to look out of the window. MR. HECKLE ENTERS LEFT and brushes off his hands. CONSTABLE and MR. FLETCHER turn to see him.)*

MR. FLETCHER: It's you again!

MR. HECKLE: Of course it's me, who else would it be? I haven't had my scones yet. *(Crosses to a chair and sits.)*

CONSTABLE: What have you done with Miss Saunders?

MR. HECKLE: Miss Saunders? Was she with you?

MR. FLETCHER: Of course she was with us. She was just here a moment ago.

MR. HECKLE: Maybe she had to leave suddenly.

CONSTABLE: Where did you come from? And where's Dr. Jekyll?

MR. HECKLE: Maybe Dr. Jekyll went somewhere with Miss Saunders. The ladies love him, you know. He's quite a catch. *(Picks up a scone, takes a bite, and begins to shake violently. Suddenly, he DISAPPEARS behind the chair, and DR. JEKYLL REAPPEARS.)*

CONSTABLE: Ah, ha! So you are the evil villain, Mr. Heckle!

DR. JEKYLL: What? What are you talking about? Who is Mr. Heckle?

MR. FLETCHER: *(Urgent.)* What have you done with Miss Saunders?

MRS. REARDON: *(ENTERS RIGHT with napkins, cheerful.)* Here we are! Napkins for everyone. Now won't you all have a nice, warm scone?

CONSTABLE: *(To MRS. REARDON.)* You! You are the mastermind behind all this evil!

MRS. REARDON: *(Innocent.)* I beg your pardon?

CONSTABLE: You have been feeding Dr. Jekyll your tainted scones every morning and turning him into the evil Mr. Heckle!

DR. JEKYLL: Mrs. Reardon, how could you? Say it isn't true!

MRS. REARDON: *(Changes into an evil, plotting woman.)* So you have uncovered my plan! It's true. I have discovered the secret to changing pure good into pure evil. Little ol' me! Just a simple housekeeper, and yet I was smarter than the great Dr. Jekyll himself! I went to the doctor's laboratory when he wasn't home, and I figured out how to make the elixir. He was too dumb to figure it out by himself!

DR. JEKYLL: Mrs. Reardon! I told you to stay away from my laboratory!

CONSTABLE: *(Takes MRS. REARDON'S arm)* That's enough of that! You're coming with us, Mrs. Reardon. Maybe you can tell us what happened to Muffy, Mrs. Fletcher, and Miss Saunders. Mr. Fletcher, seize those scones before anyone else takes a bite. *(MR. FLETCHER grabs the plate of scones and follows the CONSTABLE.)* Sorry for the inconvenience, Doctor. You won't be bothered by this villain again. *(EXITS UP LEFT through the door with MRS. REARDON and MR. FLETCHER.)*

MRS. REARDON: *(Calls back as she is dragged OFF.)* It was my discovery! I am the evil genius in this house! *(Emits a sinister laugh.)*

MR. HECKLE: *(APPEARS from behind the chair and puts his arm around the shoulder of DR. JEKYLL, who is not surprised to see him there.)* Oh, darn! We lose so many good housekeepers that way. *(DR. JEKYLL nods.)*

. . . .

16. The Ghost Explorers

RUNNING TIME: 7 minutes

CAST SIZE: 3M, 2F

CAST OF CHARACTERS

MACK.............................host of *The Ghost Explorers* television show; loves the spotlight

RONNY...........................staff technician; scaredy-cat

TERRI............................camera person; slightly afraid of ghosts

CASPER..........................friendly and mischievous ghost

MOTHER.........................Casper's mother; kind but strict

SETTING

A haunted old mansion.

PROPERTIES

Three chairs, table, vase, stationary camera, three recording devices, laptop or computer monitor, voice recorder.

The Ghost Explorers

· · · · · · ·

There are a few chairs and a table with a vase at CENTER. MACK, TERRI, and RONNY cautiously ENTER LEFT, carrying the stationary camera, a few recording devices, a laptop or computer monitor, and a voice recorder. CASPER ENTERS RIGHT simultaneously, sits in one of the chairs, and watches them with interest. He is invisible to the OTHERS. RONNY and TERRI set up the equipment around the room.

MACK: *(To the AUDIENCE, slowly, clearly, and with a sense of mystery.)* My name is Mack Rogers. I never believed in ghosts until I saw one face to face. From then on, I set out to capture what I saw on video. My team and I don't have any big camera crew with us. It's just my fellow investigators, Ronny Olson and Terri Foster. *(RONNY and TERRI nod toward the AUDIENCE, then continue setting up equipment.)* Together, we travel to the most incredibly haunted locations in the world where we spend an entire night being locked down alone, from sunset to sunrise. We are The Ghost Explorers. *(Turns to OTHERS.)* How's the set-up coming, people?

RONNY: Good, bro. I've got the full spectrum DVR cameras set around the room to record any unusual movement or apparitions.

MACK: Ronny, can you tell the folks at home why we have to use these cameras?

RONNY: Sure, Mack. These full spectrum cameras can see in the UV spectrum, the visible light spectrum, and into the infrared spectrum, so we can hopefully catch a variety of material forms. *(Intrigued, CASPER walks over to the stationary camera and stands in front of it, checking it out.)*

TERRI: *(Looks at the screen.)* Hey! I see something already! There's a mist like a white swirling form in front of the camera. *(MACK, RONNY, and CASPER run to view the screen.)* It's vanished. Let me rewind the video. *(Rewinds, then points to the screen.)* There it is! You see that? It's there, clear as day, and then it just evaporates.

MACK: Amazing! And we've only been here a few minutes. *(To the AUDIENCE.)* Tonight, we are doing a lockdown in the old Chesterfield Mansion, said to be one of the most haunted locations in the Midwest. Will we discover the unknown presence that lives in this place? Will we capture it with our highly technical instruments? *(CASPER walks up next to MACK and waves to the AUDIENCE. He then leans an arm on MACK'S shoulder. MACK reacts, frantic. CASPER is surprised and steps back.)* Did someone just touch me? Ronny, Terri, I just felt something hit my shoulder! *(To the air around him.)* Did someone just hit me? Say something! Why don't you materialize and show yourself!

TERRI: Here, Mack. Try the Spirit Box. *(Hands MACK a voice recorder. CASPER walks around and watches them, amused.)*

MACK: *(To the AUDIENCE.)* Ladies and gentlemen, this piece of equipment is called a Spirit Box. It is an adjustable frequency sweep device with white noise distributed between frequency steps. It is designed exclusively for paranormal enthusiasts. With this very sensitive instrument, we can receive relevant responses to specific questions. Let's see if the ghost who just hit me wants to speak to us. *(Searches around the room and speaks slowly.)* Is there anyone here who wants to say anything to Ronny, Terri, and me? *(There is no response. CASPER is intrigued, and walks up to MACK to study the device.)* You can say anything you want. Just speak into this box.

CASPER: *(Speaks into the recorder, cheerful.)* Hi there!

RONNY: *(Jumps.)* Did you just hear something? I thought I heard "out of air" in a demonic, growling voice. Play it back and listen. *(MACK pretends to rewind the machine, then plays a muffled recording of CASPER'S voice, or CASPER can speak the lines in a muffled, inconspicuous way.)*

TERRI: I heard it! It was so clear! It said, "I want bear." Maybe the ghost wants his old teddy-bear or something like that.

MACK: Let's ask him another question, see if we can draw him out a little more. *(Talks slowly.)* We only want to help you. Are you an evil ghost or a friendly ghost?

CASPER: *(Walks up to the recorder again.)* The friendliest ghost you know. *(EXPLORERS jump.)*

MACK: Did you hear that? He said, "The end of all you know."

TERRI: No, I think it was, "There are ten ghosts to go."

RONNY: No, no! I heard, "There's plenty of boats to row." Maybe he was a fisherman in a former life, and he wants to get back to the sea. *(CASPER gets an idea, picks up the vase from the table and slowly lifts it in the air. The EXPLORERS see this happening and jump into action.)*

MACK: Look at that! It's a material levitation. Are you getting this, Terri?

TERRI: *(Aims a camera at the floating vase and follows it around as CASPER moves the vase around the room.)* I'm on it, dude. *(RONNY gets scared and starts to run OFF LEFT.)*

MACK: *(Stops him.)* Ronny! Don't run! We must face this demon down. *(Speaks to the air around him.)* So you like moving things, do you? What else can you move? How about this chair? *(Shoves one of the chairs.)* Or how about this table? *(Pushes the table with his foot. CASPER puts the vase back on the table, runs to the* *full spectrum camera, and does a dance in front of it. EXPLORERS are searching the room for any signs of movement.)*

RONNY: *(Sees the white mist on the screen again as CASPER does the hula in front of the camera.)* Mack, look! The mist is back on the screen.

MACK: *(Looks at the screen, then runs in front of the camera and stands directly in front of CASPER, yelling out toward the AUDIENCE. CASPER moves his arms all around MACK, though MACK does not react.)* We know you're here! Make yourself known to us! Why don't you just materialize so we can see you? *(CASPER prances around the room, crosses to a chair, and moves it.)* Aw, come on! Is that all you got? Move something else! Prove to us that you're here! *(CASPER crosses to another chair and twirls it around. EXPLORERS are stunned. CASPER dances around. MOTHER ENTERS RIGHT and watches. EXPLORERS do not see her.)*

RONNY: Did you see that!?

TERRI: *(Scared.)* That chair lifted right off the floor and twirled around in mid-air! We better get out of here!

MACK: Are you kidding? This is the most paranormal activity we've ever witnessed! Come on! Let's check the instruments! *(EXPLORERS check their equipment and search the room.)*

MOTHER: Casper! What are you doing?

CASPER: *(Stops suddenly.)* Nothing.

MOTHER: Casper? Tell me the truth.

CASPER: Aw, Mom, I was just having a little fun with the TV guys.

MOTHER: What have I told you about interacting with paranormal investigators?

CASPER: *(Ashamed.)* Don't play around with them.

MOTHER: *(Stern.)* Why?

CASPER: *(Still ashamed, like he's heard it a hundred times before.)* 'Cause if they think our house is haunted, they'll never leave us alone.

MOTHER: That's right. Now get yourself to bed. It's late.

CASPER: Aw, Mom. Just one more little prank? These guys are really awesome.

MOTHER: You go to bed this instant! *(CASPER EXITS RIGHT. MOTHER walks up beside MACK, smiles, and waves to the AUDIENCE.)*

MACK: *(To AUDIENCE.)* Well, ladies and gentlemen, the activity that was so incredibly strong just a moment ago seems to have disappeared suddenly. But we are going to stay here, locked down in this haunted place all night, to capture proof of our paranormal experiences. So stay tuned, because we are...

MACK/TERRI/RONNY: *(Together, to the AUDIENCE.)* ... The Ghost Explorers! *(MOTHER still smiles and waves to the AUDIENCE.)*

• • • • • • •

Production Notes

All scenes may be adapted for gender flexibility by changing pronouns and names to a reasonable degree when necessary. It is also perfectly acceptable to have girls play male roles or vice versa, which can even provide additional humorous effect.

All scenes are designed to teach basic acting principles and give actors a range of experiences. Elaborate stage settings are not necessary. Basic sets and props will work fine for the purpose of learning, especially when the scenes are used in a classroom setting. Staging ideas have been suggested to help with more elaborate productions. In most cases, a couple of chairs and a sturdy table will be the maximum set necessary.

Developing props and costumes for these scenes can be creative and fun, and the students can really use their imaginations when it comes to collaborating on the needed props. Working to bring out the humorous aspects of each scene can be a catalyst for very creative ideas.

Specific Suggestions for Producing Each Scene

1. YOU COMPLETE ME

    Use an appliance box with a hole cut in the top to fit Mr. Winkowski's head, and place a stool inside the box so the actor is seated comfortably. Ask your students to design a funny logo for Dr. Madd on the front of the box. Next to Mr. Winkowski, it can be comical to have a table covered with "Mad Scientist" paraphernalia. Let your imagination be your guide! The hair dryer used to thaw Mr. Winkowski's head is a fun bit. If possible, make the hair dryer actually turn on, but be careful not to get the heat too close to the actor's head. This prop can be pantomimed but has a great effect if it is actually blowing air to thaw the head. If you can, use a blue light or spotlight to highlight the holograms. Adding a few costume pieces can really bring this scene to life.

2. HOW TIME FLIES

This scene takes place in an outdoor setting near an ocean or bay. A painted backdrop for this scenic setting adds great effect (sheets work well and are the cheapest fabric you can buy!), but pantomiming the setting works, too. Create a hand-held box with wires and knobs to serve as the time machine, or repurpose any outdated electronics you may have laying around. Deck the pirates out in full regalia to contrast with the contemporary scientists.

3. BUNK MATES

This scene requires a strong table to act as Jesse's bed, and there should be enough space underneath the "bed" to house the monster comfortably. It can be fun to have the monster's "house" decorated like a little apartment that is revealed once we meet the monster. Sheets and a pillow are necessary to maintain the illusion of Jesse's bed.

4. YOU DON'T SAY

I have produced this scene with three dog "kennels" made out of PVC pipe (because of a very energetic parent) and it was fun for both actors and audience, but the kennels can also be pantomimed if necessary. You can use simple ears, touches of fur on hats, and a few human costume pieces to identify the different dogs.

5. AN UNEXPECTED VISITOR

   For this scene, create a glowing campfire with wood, sticks and an orange lightbulb for No-Duh's camp. Beside the campfire, set a small table with rustic bowls and utensils. The actor playing No-Duh should wear kneepads along with a large robe that covers his feet and legs, and the actor playing Duke can use a toy light saber to fight off the giant mosquitoes and show No-Duh his combat moves.

6. THREE HEADS ARE BETTER THAN ONE

   This scene is a bit short for a full-on movie theater set, so using a podium for the ticket seller and a table for concessions counter is much easier. However, creative costuming can add a lot to this scene. Construct a giant t-shirt for your three "monster" actors to wear, so that the students experience working together as one unit. Sharing a huge, simply-designed t-shirt with three head holes and two sleeves is a great way to encourage teamwork, and it's also hilarious to watch! Audiences love this humorous element.

7. THE NUTS AND BOLTS OF CHARM SCHOOL

   The three robots in this scene can be portrayed with simple silver vests and hats. You can also make a more elaborate statement by using flexible, silver duct pipes for arms and metallic fabric for bodies. The actors' movements and monotonous voices will be the key to creating the robotic characters.

8. READY, SET, DUEL

   This scene takes place in a forest setting which can be created or imagined, so all you really need are a couple of sticks and plenty of room to move. Long wizard beards and big, floppy hats are an added bonus.

9. HAPPY BIRTHDAY, CAPTAIN DIRK

When setting this scene, make sure the actors are all facing the audience as they work at their various stations. Use a few tables to serve as their terminals, and if you wish you can get a little more elaborate by adding keyboards for a few of the actors and a swivel chair for Captain Dirk. The invisible screen, which is also the fourth wall facing the audience, acts as a strong point of concentration for the actors.

10. THE AMOEBA

This scene can be very simply produced. If possible, create a 1950s look with costume pieces to compliment the style of the movie trailer. To portray the Amoeba in the end of the scene, connect as many actors as you can into one giant, writhing blob.

11. THERE'S NO PLACE LIKE HOME

This scene lends itself to either basic or elaborate set design. The spaceship is offstage, so the setting can simply be rock formations and sand. Creating some humorous "spacesuits" will add to the characters.

12. WHAT KIND OF GHOUL AM I?

This scene takes place in a modest domestic setting, therefore a couple of chairs and a coffee table will suffice. The addition of fake fangs and even a cape for Mr. Ghoul can add to the humor. If using fangs, don't allow them to hinder the actor's speech and make sure he practices clear enunciation.

13. SUPER-DUPER HEROS

Use a few costume pieces to indicate each super-hero's signature outfit, and feel free to use wild and colorful props. The sky's the limit on your creativity! This scene can be staged in a simple black-box setting or a more elaborate secret hideout.

14. THAT OLD SILK HAT

   This scene takes place in a winter wonderland. Gloves, hats, and scarves give the suggestion that the weather outside is frightful. The character of Chilly will need a top hat and might be dressed all in white.

15. HECKLE OR JEKYLL?

   This scene takes place in an interior house setting. Two chairs and a table are all the furniture necessary, and make sure that one of the chairs big enough for an actor to hide behind. The window and door can be pantomimed with careful blocking. Time and budget permitting, you can add costume pieces to create a Victorian feel.

16. THE GHOST EXPLORERS

   This scene takes place in an abandoned house that is thought to be haunted. This gives great opportunity for a "spooky" set design. Cover chairs and furniture with white sheets for a deserted effect, and string cobwebs around the room to create that "unlived-in look". The Ghost Explorers should have a few cameras or small boxes that can be used as wireless monitors. Keep it simple or go all out. Have fun!

ABOUT THE AUTHOR

Jan Peterson Ewen has been steeped in theater since she first received her Musical Theater degree in Southern California in 1978. She performed in the Los Angeles area for ten years then moved back north with her young family.

Jan was a founder of Western Washington Center for the Arts in Port Orchard and has served as its Artistic Director for the past fifteen years. She has directed well over sixty musicals and plays and has a special heart for developing actors of all ages.

Jan has been excited to utilize her love of writing to create original acting material. She has workshopped her ideas with her students and has created scenes that are fun to perform while developing specific acting skills and critical techniques.

Writing for the theater has taken other forms for Jan, as well. She recently published her first novel, *Starring on Bay Street*, which is a fictitious story about the life of a local theater with all its quirky characters and humorous happenings.

Jan lives in the lush, green Puget Sound region of Washington with her talented husband Bruce, who provides all the music for their theatrical endeavors. Bruce and Jan share three amazing adult children, who are the joys of their life.

Check out Jan's website at www.JanPetersonEwen.com for more information on her novel as well as additional bonus material and acting resources. Follow Jan on Twitter at @actingscenes and on Facebook at www.facebook.com/ActingScenes.